Healthcare Quality & Productivity
Practical Management Tools

Roey Kirk, M.S.M.

AN ASPEN PUBLICATION®
Aspen Publishers, Inc.

1988

Rockville, Maryland
Royal Tunbridge Wells

Library of Congress Cataloging-in-Publication Data

Kirk, Roey.
Healthcare quality & productivity

Includes bibliographical references.
1. Health facilities--Personnel management--Handbooks, manuals, etc. 2. Health facilities--Personnel management--Forms. 3. Medical care--Quality control--Handbooks, manuals, etc. 4. Medical care--Quality control--Forms. 5. Health services administration--Forms. I. Title. II. Title: Healthcare quality and productivity. III. Title: Health care quality & productivity. [DNLM: 1. Delivery of Health Care--economics--United States. 2. Delivery of Health Care--organization & administration--United States. 3. Health Services--organization & administration--United States. 4. Quality of Health Care--economics--United States. W 84 AA1 K5h]
RA971.35.K57 1988   362.1′1′068   88-10397
ISBN: 0-87189-786-5

Library of Congress Catalog Card Number: 88-10397
ISBN: 0-87189-786-5

Printed in the United States of America

1 2 3 4 5

Table of Contents

Section 5
Leadership: The Key to Quality & Productivity Results 67

Section 6
Ideas for Improving Quality & Productivity 83

Section 7
Glossary of Formulas & Data Collection Forms 97

Preface

Today, healthcare providers live in a competitive, cost-constrained environment; and the issue of quality has become a matter of financial and organizational survival. Achieving both a desirable level of quality and a level of productivity sufficient to contain costs often seems like conflicting objectives to healthcare managers. Too often we throw up our hands (and other things too) in frustration, unaware of simple solutions that can lead to accomplishing both of these objectives.

The purpose of this workbook is to provide systems, methods, and techniques for healthcare managers and administrators to help them manage their units, departments, and divisions more effectively and more efficiently with the indirect, but ultimate, focus on improving patient care. This book is filled with practical management tools that have been used successfully and taught to thousands of students, managers, and administrators. It doesn't just tell how you *should* do things; instead, it provides forms and formulas that can be copied and implemented immediately. The goal is not to tie up your time recreating an idea from the book, but to give you the opportunity to quickly try out an idea and assess its potential application in your organization.

The step-by-step instruction style enables both independent and classroom learning. Practicing healthcare managers and administrators will find this an excellent resource for new ideas, innovations, and challenges that will help them manage their responsibilities. In addition, key concepts, formulas, and forms have been set up so that educators of healthcare management and administration students can easily make overhead transparencies and homework assignments directly from the book examples. Each form and worksheet is set up two ways: (1) first as a sample, filled in to show how it is used, and (2) as a blank form ready for copying. The forms are also available on software, compatible with Apple's Macintosh™ hardware, from the author (Roey Kirk Associates, Healthcare Management Consultants, P.O. Box 160309, Miami, Florida 33116), for those of you who want to revise or personalize the forms.

Although the outline of the book follows a process that is best understood when read in order, the text has also been designed to meet the needs of readers who only want to read a particular section. In Section 1, *Introduction: Managing Quality & Productivity Together*, the basic concepts of quality and productivity are discussed with an emphasis on quality as the key ingredient and baseline information for the productivity process. Drawing on information from a time-valued classification system, Section 2, *Productivity: A Quality-based Approach*, shows how to use the unit of service in combination with a time-valued acuity classification system to define productivity standards as targets for individual departments and specialties.

Section 3, *Reallocating Employees to Meet Variable Demand*, shows how to use identified productivity targets daily, on a shift-by-shift basis, as a tool to help healthcare managers make staffing decisions. Staff is prescheduled for the average expectation of volume and acuity; however, both volume- and acuity-related variations can occur and cannot be ignored if quality and productivity standards are to be met on an ongoing basis. When such a day arrives, managers need a can't-fail system to assist them in making reallocation decisions in a methodical, qualitative, and cost-efficient way. In Section 4, *Monitoring, Evaluation, & Control*, simple, quality-based productivity systems that can be used to monitor and evaluate both quality and productivity performance prospectively, concurrently, and retrospectively are described.

In Section 5, *Leadership: The Key to Quality & Productivity Results*, quality and productivity management are examined from the perspective of the leader, who is ultimately responsible for both. It is the manager who is accountable, not only for the systems but also for the motivation and participation of his or her employees. An outstanding leader can bring out a multitude of creative and innovative ideas and make it more fulfilling for staff to come to work. Results of this belief are shared in Section 6, *Ideas for Improving Quality & Productivity*. Finally, something I wished for when I started my management career, *Glossary of Formulas & Data Collection Forms*, is provided in Section 7.

This was a particularly special book to write because I have literally thousands of coauthors. I started developing this material for a course entitled, Applied Management in Healthcare Organizations which I taught from 1980 to 1986 at Florida International University. Since that time I've used it to teach thousands more in workshops and seminars. Almost every time I've taught this material a participant has asked a question, made an observation, challenged me, caught an error in mathematics (almost always), or made a criticism. Every time I was smart enough to listen to that person, the material improved. If you are one of those people, know that I am grateful and thank you.

Roey Kirk, M.S.M.

Section 1

Introduction:
Managing Quality & Productivity Together

Many healthcare managers in the field today are shaking their heads and wondering, "How did I get *here*? All I wanted to do was save a few lives and deliver high-quality patient care." Oddly enough, some of those people became managers because they accomplished those objectives and with a superior level of expertise. Clinical or technical staff members with a high level of performance are ideal candidates for the position of manager in their department because of their experience, skills, and knowledge. Although there were many nontechnical aspects to the manager's position the expectation from senior management was that the high-achieving "winners" would be winners in their managerial role as well.

Pressure from tightening cost constraints and fierce competition from many directions occasionally make the *challenge* of healthcare management seem death defying. In some states rate setting or capitation schemes are being considered; and, in the private sector, third party payers, our own physicians, and community businesses are all competing with traditional healthcare services for a share of the healthcare dollar. In response to a crush of changes, healthcare managers are rising to the occasion, looking for information that will enable them to manage quality patient care and productivity in delivering care so that they, their departments, and their institution can survive in the marketplace.

We can no longer set quality goals without consideration for what the cost will be. Nor can we strive for productivity targets that will not allow us to maintain an adequate level of quality.
Healthcare quality and productivity will have to work together or they won't work at all.

Healthcare organizations have somewhat of an edge in the area of quality and productivity management because the end-stage goal, patient care, is very clear and usually supported by everyone who works in the organization.   Every employee is there for the patient. Some give **direct patient care** (e.g., laboratory personnel, technicians, dietitians, nurses, respiratory therapists); others provide **indirect care, or related services** (e.g., maintenance engineers; personnel in environmental services, public relations and marketing, data processing) supporting those who provide direct patient care. Both groups are equally important to and responsible for positively impacting on healthcare quality and productivity.

Quality:

1. that which makes something what it is; characteristic element; atttribute. 2. basic nature; kind; character. 3. the degree of excellence a thing possesses. 4. excellence; superiority.

Productivity:

1. the action of producing abundantly; fertile. 2. marked by abundant production. 3. of or engaged in the creating of economic value, or the producing of goods and services.

Managing quality of patient care or a related service on one hand, and budget and productivity on the other, can create conflict for healthcare managers, especially if they are approached as two separate activities. However, approaching both activities together (1) facilitates achievement of both, (2) makes it more logical, and (3) makes it easier. We no longer work in an environment where we can set quality goals without consideration for what the cost will be. On the other hand, maintaining budget and productivity targets that are too tight to enable an adequate level of quality won't work either. Consumers (including patients, physicians, and third party payers) are gaining access to quality outcome information, and there's no amount of cost savings that will draw them to a healthcare provider who has gained a reputation for poor performance and substandard quality.

Workbook at-a-Glance

This workbook focuses on the goal of managing and maintaining both quality and productivity. It contains many ideas and methods, and forms that can be copied and used. The objective is to provide resource materials for working managers, both new and experienced, and students of healthcare management who want to know what happens in *real life*. We can hand this responsibility over to "management experts," but we can't do it and maintain clinical and technical quality levels we need to survive successfully. The department-level clinical and technical experts, armed with budget and productivity support systems, are the best people to implement and maintain systems that optimize quality and productivity.

Quality and productivity really can be accomplished, and with relative ease. Everything in this workbook is designed to provide healthcare managers with useful information that will enable them to maintain the desired level of quality under ever-increasing cost constraints. In the past, healthcare providers relied on volume and price increases to improve operating revenues so that staffing could remain as high as possible. However, competition and rate controls have restricted these avenues; and now, because of the high percentage of dollars spent on labor, productivity improvements have even greater potential for positively affecting operating expenses. Productivity increases are possible if quality goals are maintained and enhanced concurrently. The following approach will be used in this workbook as we work toward optimizing both quality and productivity:

- **Define the desired level of quality**

    In theory, this task is easy because everyone wants "optimal"[1] quality. It becomes more difficult, in practice, as theories are defined and committed to paper through policies, procedures, standards of care and performance, and patient care plans. This subject will be addressed only slightly as the author is not a clinical or technical expert in the variety of fields that will be represented by managers using this workbook. There are many fine texts dealing with clinical and technical quality levels; there are less on the systems managers can use to identify, define, and implement quality levels and those systems will be discussed later in the section.

- **Calculate the budget required to achieve the desired level of quality**

    Once a predetermined level of quality is defined, we must be able to answer the question, What is this going to cost? If we can't answer, we'll

---

[1] Optimal—the best or most favorable degree, condition, or amount—as opposed to maximal—the greatest quantity, number, or degree possible or permissible.

have no idea whether or not we can afford to provide that level of quality. In labor-intensive departments we can get a pretty good idea about cost just by looking at salary budgets. However, there are other costs to consider, such as equipment, rental fees, medical and office supplies, and maintenance and repair. If we are going to optimize quality within our cost constraints, we must be able to identify the cost of our desired level of quality.

- **Plan for providing the desired level of quality within (or in spite of) the cost constraint**

Most healthcare managers know what they want in terms of quality, even if it's not yet defined or documented. And most know, generally, what achieving it will cost. Problems arise from wanting to do more than can be afforded in the budget. Resolving this issue is the purpose of this workbook.

Quality First, Then Productivity

Quality *and* productivity can be compatible and can be accomplished. To achieve this objective, managers need to know (1) what quality is in their department and (2) how to manage it effectively and efficiently. Managers may wonder how to measure quality; how to quantify quality; how to ensure it on a daily basis. These are tough questions; but, fortunately, there are specific and simple methodologies that can lead to their answers. The first step in all of these methods is to define a predetermined level of quality that is acceptable to everyone, including the patient.

The influence of Madison Avenue, the advertising center of America (now pushing steadily into healthcare marketing agendas), has etched indelible perceptions about quality in our minds. External sources in our society condition us to believe that if you want quality, you have to pay for it. You've all heard, or read, television, radio, and magazine advertisements that imply or state outright that you get what you pay for, or that you have to spend money to make money. In healthcare, we've bought into that theory by increasing staffing levels and paying top dollar for supplies and equipment. There are myths that we, as healthcare providers and managers, will have to question and overcome if we want to survive financially:

- Quality myth #1: The more quality you want, the more it's going to cost.
- Quality myth #2: There is no such thing as too much quality.
- Quality myth #3: Quantity leads to quality...more is better.

When you think about the above within your own department, you can see why they are referred to as myths; yet, some, or all, of those statements are adhered to, often with enthusiasm, in hospitals and healthcare agencies. What are some of the factors that lead us to believe a product or service is one of quality? Here are some examples:

- In a *quality* clothing store more sales staff may be on duty to reduce waiting time and provide more time and personal attention for the customers.

- In the same clothing store fabrics may be selected that are more valuable or durable; garments may be completely lined and sewn with larger seams to aid alteration.

- Customers may be given the option of (1) waiting while their alterations are completed or (2) having the finished garment delivered to them at their home.

All the above services are provided for an additional cost to someone, usually the consumer. More sales staff, better quality and extra fabric, an on-location seamstress and sewing machine , and a delivery van and driver all cost money. In each of these cases the cost of the resources (labor, supplies, equipment) contributed to the ultimate designation of quality—the extra touch. It is a common, but sometimes incorrect, assumption that the more resources used to deliver a product or service, the more qualitative and costly it becomes. Resources are often referred to as the *3 Ms,* representing *man* (labor), *materials* (supplies), and *machinery* (capital equipment). They all have one thing in common—they all cost *money.*

Quality, however, doesn't always cost more. It can cost a lot more to track down the source of a problem (reference: endless, expensive meetings), pay the legal settlement (errors can lead to lawsuits), or implement the changes, than it would have cost to do it the right way in the first place. In one hospital management started to log the actual cost of meetings, patient complaints, and followup related to the need for a hospitalwide patient transportation system and came to the conclusion that it would cost far less to implement the new system than it was costing to problem solve and work around it.

Because most problems regarding quality are built into our systems, policies, and procedures, management can take a leadership role in building *solutions* into those same systems, policies, and procedures. Employees can be a trememdous help here. They know what's wrong; and, just as often, they know how to fix it, even prevent it. Why doesn't management do...? is a frequent question staff members ask. We need to tap our staff members as "expert" resources because they have the answers to quality and productivity challenges. They want to deliver quality care and services. They want to be able to complete 8 hours of work in 8 hours, not 10. And we need quality just as much as productivity to survive in the current healthcare market.

Is Perceived Quality Real Quality?

A related issue of quality for healthcare managers is consumer perception. Through marketing studies it has been shown that consumers expect to have their *lives saved* by healthcare providers, assuming their physicians wouldn't practice at an institution that delivered substandard care. They form their perceptions around things, such as the food, the way they are treated, the cleanliness of their surroundings, and the speed with which their needs are met, all of which frustrate their caregivers, who are trying to focus attention on *real quality issues.* Even though being nice to Mrs. Jones or making the meal tray look nicer won't save her life, that service makes a big difference to the patient, and ultimately to the competitive health of the organization. The push for competition at the same time costs are being cut or scrutinized generates additional workload and responsibility for many healthcare managers; however, both perceived and real issues regarding quality must be considered.

We can deal with both issues by talking to physicians, patients, patients' families, and our own staff members and asking them a few simple, but crucial questions:

- What do we want patient care or related service outcomes to be (clinical standards of care, technical service standards, client satisfaction standards)?

- What will the clinician, technician, and/or employee do to facilitate achievement of these goals (performance standards)?

- How long will it take for each of them to provide this service (quality-based productivity standards)?

- What will the patient do to demonstrate that desired outcomes have been achieved, or how will results be measured?

Ideally, when we look at quality, concurrently or retrospectively, we want to be able to assess whether or not standards have been met, exceeded, or not been met. If we have met the standard, then we're on the right track; but if a standard has not

Care Standard Patient Care or Service Outcomes	Performance Standard Employee Responsibilities	Resource Standard Quality-Based Productivity Target
Patient will be prepared for discharge with specific plans for coping with pain at home. The plan will consist of continuing with all prescribed techniques for coping with pain. Patient will be able to state appropriate reasons to contact physician. Patient will be able to state side effects of prescribed medication.	Prior to discharge the clinical representative will review the following information with the patient and question the patient to assure comprehension: • Medication: prescriptions, schedule, procedures, and potential complications • Physical restrictions list • Related dietary goals • Possibility of, and plans for, coping with a temporary setback	**.75 hours** (staff care hours per patient discharge) *Resource standards identify how many labor hours are needed to deliver a predetermined level of quality care. They also provide clinical staff with productivity targets.*

Educational example only. More specific information will be needed for use in your department or facility.

been met, then we must ask whether it was due to our process—the way we do things (performance standards). Remember, the purpose of measuring and monitoring quality is not to play "I gotcha." The purpose is to ensure that quality services are always being given—that individuals know their role and responsibility in delivering quality—and if they're not, to fix them immediately and develop new systems to prevent future breakdown. The chart above displays an example of how this concept can be applied.

Standards of Care, Performance, & Resources

In the example above, and in the **Care • Performance • Resource Plan**, Form 1.1, on the next page, the patient **care standards** are goals, clearly stated in terms of specific, measurable outcomes. Expectations should be clarified and agreed to by the patient, his or her family, and the caregiver to ensure the best chance for success. The **performance standards** clearly state staff member responsibilities, what his or her role will be in helping the patient achieve designated goals. For example, the patient should be able to state appropriate reasons for contacting (or not) the physician and the professional staff will be responsible for reviewing the information with the patient and questioning the patient to assure comprehension.

Care Standard Patient Care or Service Outcomes	Performance Standard Employee Responsibilities	Resource Standard Quality-Based Productivity Target
Social Services: Patient will have knowledge of community resources available after discharge.	The social worker will (1) evaluate (initially and ongoing) the patient who will need referral to community agencies after discharge; (2) alert the physician to the patient's need for community referral; and (3) introduce the patient and/or the patient's family to available services.	**1.0 hours total**
Physical Therapy: Patient will learn appropriate exercises and correct method so they can participate in a daily exercise program during inpatient stay and after discharge.	The physical therapist will provide patient with information about their independent, ongoing therapeutic self-exercise program, as prescribed, including; (1) demonstration, (2) pictures, and (3) verbal instruction.	**2.5 hours total**
Occupational Therapy: Patient will learn to use energy-saving techniques that will enable them to increase endurance and activity tolerance to _____ .	The occupational therapist will (1) teach energy saving techniques and practices and (2) show how to simplify a work setting, structure a day, and prioritize activities.	**1.5 hours total**
Therapeutic Recreation: Patient will carry over appropriate leisure activities after discharge and have a written plan, including a list of activities, for continuing activities at home.	The therapeutic recreation therapist will work with patient on a plan to continue pursuing interests and/or new leisure activities at home.	**1.0 hours total (5 group visits)**
Nutritional Services: Patient will lose ____ pounds to attain ideal body weight and maintain weight loss ongoing.	The dietitian will (1) provide a well-balanced _____ calorie diet, which will include all food groups, and (2) reinforce physical therapy's exercise and fitness program, explaining how it can also help patient reduce.	**1.5 hours total**

Educational example
More specific information will be needed for use in your department or facility.

Care • Performance • Resource Plan

Resource Standard Quality-Based Productivity Target	**Performance Standard** Employee Responsibilities	**Care Standard** Patient Care or Service Outcomes

Care • Performance • Resource Plan

Form 1.1

Finally, there must be a **resource standard** that identifies how many hours (or fraction) are required (and, hopefully, budgeted) to achieve the performance standard. All three standards must be compatible for the system to work. If the standards of care in a department are unrealistically high, without a corresponding number of resources, no amount of fine performance by staff members will help patients achieve their goals. To achieve quality there must be (1) an acceptance of what quality is; (2) a specific process that will, with some degree of certainty, lead staff members toward achieving the predetermined level of quality; and (3) sufficient staff available to accomplish this on an ongoing basis. We are responsible for managing in a cost-contained, labor-intensive environment, where there are only two choices for survival...*increased productivity or decreased profits*. If we continue to probe for ways to deliver optimal quality care and services within productivity and financial constraints we will be in the best possible position to integrate and achieve all three of these standards.

The answers to quality and productivity questions lie, to a large extent in the standards. If we can identify what we want for those who use our service, and how to measure the outcomes, then we can manipulate different methods and productivity efforts, evaluating them on two counts: (1) Did we save time and maximize our efficiency? and (2) Were we able to do so while maintaining the agreed on level of quality? The **Care • Performance • Resource Plan**, Form 1.1, shown on the previous two pages, displays a variety of standards. In each case there is

---

Standards

Care: Identify what we want to accomplish

Performance: Describe specific staff member actions

Resource: Target staff hours required to achieve the predetermined care standard

Target the standard of care by defining the acceptable level of quality and then budget for the resources (labor, supplies, equipment) that will enable your staff to maintain or exceed that target

(1) an expected patient outcome that contributes to a predetermined level of quality; (2) a process caregivers are expected to follow; and (3) an expected amount of time that the task(s) should take. In many healthcare organizations that amount of time is being trimmed, even sliced, but the expectation of process and patient care outcomes has remained unchanged. No wonder some employees go home at night feeling like they haven't done their best at providing care for patients or services to their coworkers in other departments. They are trying to do more with less, and their idea of flexible staffing is stretching themselves beyond their limits to continually produce more.

That is not to say that there haven't been any inefficiencies in healthcare organizations over the years; certainly, there have been. But those days are moving farther into the past; and, today, most managers are concerned with knowing *when* productivity efforts have been maximized. Using the **Care • Performance • Resource Plan** will help your own staff members analyze patient care priorities or service demands and continually reevaluate department quality goals in light of, and within, current productivity constraints. Its use will enable them to share, as experts in their field, their collective knowledge regarding the most efficient way to meet designated patient care or service outcomes and reach consensus about how long it *should* take to complete the action(s). Professional staff will never get excited about productivity, but they will always get excited about quality. If they know, up front, that they have only a specific amount of time to complete a procedure, they can plan ahead to focus on the most important aspects of care that will enable them to maximize quality within the time constraint. Conversely, if the procedure can't be done, they can address why not and describe the potential consequences.

Whenever there is a standard , there is the potential for objective evaluation. If we had a data base for information, we could use the sample standards displayed in the **Care • Performance • Resource Plan** to objectively evaluate whether we:

- met the standard
- exceeded the standard
- did not meet the standard[2]

If a standard is written correctly, but it has not been met, then it should be clear from reading the standard (1) why not and (2) how to fix it. In the nutritional services section of Form 1.1-Example, the patient care standard or goal is for the patient to lose an agreed on amount of weight and maintain that weight loss. The

---

[2] I will always be indebted to Art Worth, management consultant, for introducing me to this concept and freeing me, forever, from words like meritorious, superior, acceptable, average, and, worst of all, below average.

patient may or may not meet that goal, or may do exceptionally well and lose more weight and become more physically fit than anticipated. If the goal is not met, however, it could be because of something the patient did (such as having secret chocolate bar breaks) or the caregiver did (such as delivering trays with incorrect calorie counts). Either our process was wrong or the process was right, but someone—one of our staff or the patient—didn't follow it. If the (1) performance standard has proved to be sound, (2) the dietitian did everything he or she was supposed to do, (3) spot checks of trays indicate correct portions and calories, and (4) physical exercise program has been maintained, then we have to probe further. That's when we may find out about the chocolate bar breaks. Regardless of whether the unmet goal is a result of the chocolate breaks or one of the other factors, such as inconsistent portions or calories on patient trays, we have the information we need to focus on correcting the situation.

What Is Productivity?

Many healthcare professionals are committed to doing everything they can when it comes to delivering services to both patients and other departments; but that usually takes time, something we no longer have in unlimited quantities. As time constraints continue to be tightened, we must determine, by asking those employees who provide a service, whether or not the activities that consume their time also are the most important in terms of quality outcomes. Airline flight attendants may be able to get away with saying, "This is a no-frills airline now," when they throw a bag of peanuts on what you were sure was going to be your lunch tray. Healthcare providers can't. We must work at maximal productivity, and meet the challenge of providing the highest quality care, feasible within existing cost constraints. Quality standards, developed to be compatible with existing productivity targets/constraints, can help us achieve this goal.

In many institutions budget dollars are not available to match the desired standard of care. Quality goals are set and performance standards are identified; but, when the performance translates into labor hours, it becomes clear that available dollars are insufficient to pay for targeted resources (labor, supplies, equipment). That's why the issue of productivity is so important. To apply this to a simple example, a manager may identify 10 hours of workload but may only be able to obtain the budget dollars to pay for 8 hours of staff. The manager can't expect the employee to try to deliver 10 hours of workload in 8 hours (although it's been done) but there are other options. Maybe there is 2 hours of activities that are unrelated to our patient care or service outcomes and we're doing these activities just because we always have. Maybe internal problems with systems, equipment, and services are stealing 2 hours per work day. Only the people who work in the department know for sure what's helping them be productive and what's standing in their way of getting work accomplished. Just as with quality, there are often misconceptions about productivity. In the illustration below comments frequently expressed by employees, when they hear the word productivity, are shown.

True or False
Increasing productivity means...

...hospital gains profits/efficiency at staff expense   __F__

...reduced staffing, cut budgets, and lost jobs   __F__

...unreasonable workloads and nonstop pace   __F__

...lower quality of service   __F__

...reduced level of job performance   __F__

...increased volume and revenue   __F__

...being observed, monitored, and timed by   __F__
     engineers or consultants with stopwatches

While some managers believe these myths too, others have learned through experience that when a group of staff members understand the positive significance of productivity it can make a difference between financial survival and failure, particularly in an environment where pricing increases are frozen in response to regulation or competition. Managers and their staff members working together have the best opportunity to achieve both quality and cost-containment goals.

Efficiency is doing things right.
Effectiveness is doing the right things.
And doing the wrong things less expensively
is not much help.

— Peter Drucker

Peter Drucker, one of the leading management thinkers of our time, is well known for his quote on the preceding page. Our employees, as providers of patient care and related services, know what they want in terms of quality for their customers (including patients, physicians, other departments) and they usually know how to achieve that quality. They are the ones who can define how to do the "right things" the "right way," the first time and in the shortest amount of time. We, as managers, need to inspire them and channel their knowledge into creating systems that will capture information that can ultimately be used to benefit patients.

Getting Staff Involved

Even though the statements in the **True or False** illustration on the previous page indicates that staff members aren't too crazy about productivity, it doesn't mean they don't want to participate in the development of departmental standards, even if those standards have to be productive. Because of the myths, or because it's just not their orientation, they may not be so quick to come up with ideas about how to do things faster, or more efficiently. But staff members are the ones who have answers to the questions below about quality and productivity. They know what's right, what's wrong, what's best for their patients; and they'll quickly come up with targets for quality. And, as important, they know how to fix things (even before they break) and make the most of their available time.

Quality & Productivity	
What's Wrong	**What's Right**
How can we fix it?	How can we maintain it?
How can we prevent it from happening again?	Can we do it better …or faster?
Can we do it better …or faster?	Can we do more of what we're doing right?

The purpose of this section was to establish clearly in the reader's mind that a pre-determined, defined, and accepted level of quality must be in place before productivity is even discussed. First, we must be familiar with what we want for our patients, or service users, and what our role will be in achieving that goal. Then, we can identify the most efficient way to achieve it. Cutting corners here could make some of the aforementioned myths become unfortunate realities. As you read this workbook, know that **each time the concept of productivity is mentioned, the underlying assumption is that the quality targets are in place, can be relied on, and will be maintained.**

In a cost-contained, labor-intensive environment, there are only two choices for survival...increased productivity or decreased profits. Reduced quality is not one of the listed options for two reasons: (1) We care about our patients and the people who use our services; and (2) Quality is the pivotal competition point in the healthcare industry. American automobile manufacturers who continually provided less than desired quality watched their potential buyers turn to the foreign market. They had to clean up their industry and now their attention and advertisements are focused on quality, probably the only variable that will bring buyers back. When it comes to purchasing quality healthcare services there is less tolerance for less than desired quality. Once patients (or other purchasers of healthcare services) turn away from a provider because of an insufficient level of quality, it's unlikely they'll return. Quality is not transferable, for money or productivity: this will be an unwavering assumption throughout this workbook.

Quality without productivity is unaffordable.
Productivity without quality is undesirable.
Quality and productivity together
is what we must have to survive; and, yes,
it can be done!

Section 2

Productivity:
A Quality-based Approach

In a general sense, all the reasons for studying productivity boil down to just one—the patient. Healthcare institutions exist, according to their mission statements, to provide quality healthcare to patients in need of services they provide. Those services may be direct patient care (physical therapy, radiology, outpatient surgery, etc.) or they may be indirect services (personnel, maintenance, public relations, etc.) to individuals, or departments who deliver direct patient care. Standards describe a predetermined and agreed on level of quality, and managers coordinate the resources. But it takes a secure financial position (i.e., money) to make quality happen. The institutions that are able to recover their costs of providing a desired level of quality will be the ones with a financially secure position and the competitive edge in the marketplace.

In today's market managers must be interested in both quality and productivity. One can't survive without the other, and an inappropriate ratio of one to the other ultimately could affect the overall survival of the institution. There is a story often told about productivity in our times, which compares the 1978 government regulation on the sale of garbage (26,911 words) to Lincoln's Gettysburg Address (268 words). We do not appear, at least from this anecdote, to be forging toward greater productivity. Yet the same government that penned the garbage regulation is mandating that healthcare costs be reduced. This action is a result of political pressure from the public, the consumers themselves who expect quality care in healthcare organizations but at a price they can afford.[3]

Wedged between the needs of the patients and the survival of the organization are patient care departments and other related service departments (who serve the

---

[3] Consumers usually do not mention quality as one of the criteria that affects their choice of institution. They expect it from all institutions. John Bilangi, vice president, American Hospital Supply, spoke on the subject of productivity in 1983. He noted that to comply with required regulatory paper work enough people would have to be hired to staff 75 hospitals, each with 250 beds, at a cost of $45 per patient per day. To the public, this probably guarantees quality care. At that cost, it should.

patients indirectly). All of the employees in these departments balance, sometimes juggle, the needs of the patients, other staff, physicians, and administration.
And sometimes, it seems, the entities they are juggling are focused on different
goals and directions (making their jobs even more pleasant). All, however, do
have something to gain from improving quality and productivity. The patient
gains by the provision of more effective and efficient use of staff time, and each
time that conscious thought is given to what is right and wrong, or what could be
done better or faster. The employee gains by feeling good about what he or she
does for patients and the organization. And the organization gains by becoming
an institution with a reputation for high-quality, cost-effective care...the opposite
of what is illustrated in the delightful caricature below.

"Cheer Up—We're Keeping Our Charges Within Government Ceilings!"

Sincere thanks to John Trever, Editorial Cartoonist for the <u>Albuquerque Journal</u> for his brilliant
rendition of our current health care situation. Healthcare executives were probably laughing
for different reasons when it was published 8 years ago. This cartoon may not be reproduced
without the permission of John Trever, <u>Albuquerque Journal</u>, P.O. Drawer "J", Albuquerque,
New Mexico 87103.

Productivity Improvement Benefits:

Productivity improvement activities can generate quality-based tools for monitoring manpower utilization in all departments, regardless of variations in volume and/or acuity.[4]

- Identifies required staff based on actual acuity classified needs
- Verifies and validates staffing requirements
- Justifies objectively skill level of department staff
- Facilitates staff allocation or reallocation based on actual patient requirements
- Reflects accurately workload and changing acuity trends

Once quality standards have been set and time values for department modalities have been identified, the information can be used for:

- Developing or monitoring patient classification systems
- Budgeting for individual departments
- Planning and prescheduling for the unknown volume and acuity
- Establishing productivity monitoring and control systems
- Generating comparative operating indicators
- Translating the bottom-line impact of the program or system

Understanding the components of quality and productivity indicators leads to successful management of costs and cost-containment efforts:

- Documents acuity levels and cost impact of each level
- Identifies areas of cost savings
- Provides performance feedback to guide future plans and decisions
- Enables comparison of each of the following to each other:

    - **Budgeted** hours per modality (HPM)
    - **Classified** hours per modality (HPM)
    - **Actual** hours per modality (HPM)

The only obstacles to achieving success in increasing productivity are:

- Determining quality standards
- Defining the unit of service
- Calculating time values per the standard unit of service
- Gaining acceptance by management and staff

---

[4] Acuity is the term used frequently in the nursing profession to describe the level of acuteness of illness; the more severe the illness or intensity of need for nursing care, the higher the acuity. Patient classification systems assist the nurse in measuring the patient's acuity level.

The quality issue was discussed in the first section, and the remaining other obstacles to increased productivity are discussed in this and following chapters. If the manager is aware of potential barriers to success, plans can be made ahead of time to reduce some of the risk involved. The philosophy, "quality isn't free, but it's less expensive than the alternatives," applies to setting up productivity and management systems too.

Getting Started on the Right Track

So, where do you start? How do you go about increasing productivity? And if it isn't any of the things that were mentioned in the "myths...," what is it? In concept, increasing productivity is easy. Basically, there are only two situations that increase productivity; and only four factors that impact on those situations:

Productivity Increases...

when the **Hours Worked**	and the **Units of Service**
Decrease	Stay the Same
Decrease Faster	Decrease
Stay the Same	Increase
Increase	Increase Faster

Of course, *doing* the above to increase productivity could be a lot harder, but it doesn't have to be. It does have to be meaningful to those who set up the system and to those who work within the system. Whenever any of these conditions exist, at the same time predetermined quality standards are achieved and maintained, productivity increases. You must be effective as well as efficient; it's not enough to be fast. Peter Drucker has a comment that relates to this:

Effectiveness is the foundation of success —
efficiency is a minimum condition for survival
after success has been achieved.
Efficiency is concerned with doing things right.
Effectiveness is doing the right things.

To optimize both quality and productivity, we must continually do the *right things the right way*. That means, for example, if we are supposed to do a specific respiratory therapy treatment *(the right thing)* three times a day, we should do that treatment the prescribed number of times and do it following department procedure *(the right way)* according to both quality and productivity indicators. A service-related example might be an environmental service aide responsible for the terminal cleaning of an ICU patient room *(the right thing)*. Because one person's perception of clean may be "no chunks of dirt" and another person's might be "sterile," it's important to define *the right way*, including indicators like (1) wipe down all furniture and fixtures, (2) strip bed, (3) vacuum, and (4) complete cleaning within 1 hour of discharge.

Standards must address both effectiveness *(the right thing)* and efficiency *(the right way)*. An effective standard—one that addresses only doing the right thing—may provide sufficient hours for patient care; but if the plan for delivery is inefficient, it will surely affect the financial viability of the department and staff members trying to achieve an unrealistic goal. Conversely, if a patient care or service hour standard is too efficient, it can inhibit an employee's ability to deliver the desired level of quality care to patients or departmets using his or her services.

Care Hours per Modality

It has already been mentioned that knowing the approved and budgeted care or service hours per modality (HPM) for the unit or department is very important when managing productivity. Sadly, in still a few remaining organizations managers subscribe to the philosophy that they do not have to concern themselves with this information.[5] For those who don't have ready access to their HPM or who just want to understand the process better, in the following pages the process will be reviewed and a form will be provided that will help in the calculation of departmental HPM, even when available information is limited.

For some healthcare managers, the discovery of this information is a real awakening. Frequently, comments include some "no wonders," such as: "No wonder I can't ever manage to schedule six people on 3-11" and "No wonder it always seems like the workload for the 7-3 RN staff is less than that for the 3-11 staff." Many facts surface because it is a system based on quantifiable input. And while it is true that you cannot make decisions about patient care and related services with only numbers, the union of quantified, validated service requirements and a manager's experienced-based judgment is usually a very successful combination.

Furthermore, some managers have made these calculations and, to their chagrin, have discovered that they had a lot less time to deliver their service. One manager of a respiratory therapy department found that after taking out fixed and nonproductive hours, there remained, on the average, only 0.35 hours (21 minutes) for direct care. Data collected by her staff indicated that, on the average, modalities required 45 minutes, including preparation and waiting time, actual direct care, and clean-up time. She made several unsuccessful attempts to justify and increase budgeted HPM to 45 minutes, and the budget committee members believed there was a real need. But, there were insufficient dollars available to fund the increase. Finally, with the help of staff members, alternate plans were made that changed the way they delivered their service. In their planning they looked at everything, and every idea was considered, as long as the quality standards were not compromised. In the end, some positive, time-saving ideas were generated: (1) use of a checklist format for charting; (2) arrangement of staffing by location to reduce travel time; and (3) negotiation with nursing staff about the best times for treatments to reduce therapist waiting time. This manager reflected that the disturbing information was worth discovering and with the help of department staff she was able to *manage* it into a positive situation for patient care.

The section on calculating budgeted HPM for a department will lead into a discussion of the role of the budgeted HPM in the staffing system as a whole and will continue to provide a perspective on the importance of this seemingly small number. This numerical representation of the available time for department staff to deliver a predetermined level of quality should be the base of every management activity and decision.

---

[5] An editorial comment here is irresistible. For success in management, it is essential that all levels of healthcare management be familiar, and fluent, in the financial and productivity aspects of their responsibilities, in addition to their clinical or technical expertise. If we don't learn how to manage our departments in this area, someone else will do it for us.

If you don't know your department's service hours per modality (HPM)...

you can calculate it yourself, if you know:

1. Total approved (budgeted) FTE.

2. Which positions are **fixed** and provide only indirect care or services.

3. Average **nonproductive** hours paid per FTE.

4. Projected modalities for the period studied (we'll be using a fiscal year).

Calculating
Hours per Modality (HPM)
Using Annual Budget Data

	26.6	**Total Annual FTEs**
−	**3.0**	**Fixed FTEs**
=	23.6	Flexible FTEs
−	**2.4**	**Nonproductive FTEs***
=	21.2	Direct FTEs
x	2080	Annual FTE Work Hours
=	44,096	Direct Care/Service Hours
÷	**44,000**	**Projected Annual Modalities**
=	**1.0**	Budgeted HPM

Bold face data represent *given* information. (*Nonproductive FTE, in this case, is *given* rather than calculated information.)

Form 2.1-Example

= *Definitions*

Projected Annual Modalities:
Expected modalities, based on historical data and prevailing external/internal variables.

2080 Hours:
Hours each FTE is paid annually (52 weeks x 40 hours/week).

Full-Time Equivalents (FTEs):
One full-time position budgeted to pay 2080 hours annually. Can be filled by one full-time worker, 2 half-time workers, or various numbers of per diem staff.

Direct FTEs:
Positions/hours devoted to direct, "hands-on" patient care or services. The direct hours provided vary according to (1) volume, (2) acuity, and (3) actual availability of staff.

Nonproductive FTEs:
Positions/hours budgeted to cover hours that are paid, but not worked. Will vary depending on approved benefits. Example:

15 vacation + 8 holidays + 6 sick x 8 hours/work day = **232 annual nonproductive hours/FTE**

232 x 21.2 department FTE + 2080 = **2.4 FTE** required to cover benefit time off

Flexible FTEs:
Volume-based (productive & nonproductive) budgeted positions.

Fixed FTEs:
Indirect care positions: managers, clerks, clinicians, etc.

Total Annual FTEs:
Includes all positions, flexible (direct), fixed, and nonproductive.

Calculating
Hours Per Modality (HPM)
Using Annual Budget Data

		Total Annual FTEs
−		**Fixed FTEs**
=		Flexible FTEs
−		**Nonproductive FTEs***
=		Direct FTEs
× 2080		Annual FTE Work Hours
=		Direct Care/Service Hours
÷		**Projected Annual Modalities**
=		Budgeted HPM

---

* This can be calculated two different ways. #1: Last fiscal year's actual hours + 2080. #2: Projected nonproductive hours **per FTE** + 2080 x total flexible FTEs (above) = annual nonproductive FTE. **Bold face data represent** *given* **information.**

Form 2.1

The Resource (Cost) Management System

By now, you should have a clear concept of what your care or service HPM are and how they evolve.[6] Ideally, information in departmental logs and classification data provide the documentation of hours needed; and, in the best case, the budgeted HPM should reflect the average intensity, or acuity. We all know too well that as cost constraints get tighter and inpatients get sicker, required resources needed to provide quality care may simply be at a cost too high for the institution to bear and still remain financially stable. Thus, in the paradox of what is needed versus what is affordable, the healthcare manager must understand and be able to analyze the department HPM as a representation of availability of service and carry with him or her a commitment to both quality and cost effectiveness.

According to Peters and Waterman, excellent companies stay close to the customer, discovering what purchasers want and need, and then giving it to them.[7] A revelation? Not really; at least not to those who provide patient care.

The award-winning book, <u>In Search of Excellence</u>, by Thomas Peters and Robert Waterman, Jr., should be required reading for all healthcare managers. In the book, the authors showed how managers at 62 of the nation's best-run companies differ from their colleagues at lesser firms. They found that at the "excellent" companies there was a belief in service and quality, and people were valued as individuals. Healthcare managers who read this book will probably be amazed at how closely their departments match Peters and Waterman's descriptions of "excellent" firms, even though they do not specifically address the healthcare industry. In addition, as they discuss a brief list of commonalities among the 62 firms, one item, staying close to the customer, is something many healthcare providers have always done extremely well. Other industries are just now catching up to the healthcare industry in the present obsessive pursuit of quality.

---

[6] For more indepth information on these calculations and other labor utilization issues, see the companion workbook: Roey Kirk, *Healthcare Staffing & Budgeting: Practical Management Tools.* (Rockville, Md.: Aspen Publishers, Inc., 1988).

[7] Thomas Peters and Robert Waterman, Jr., *In Search of Excellence* (New York: Harper & Row Publishers, 1982).

Managing via the unit of service is the most thorough and effective way to pursue both quality and cost-containment goals. The illustration of the staffing system on page 30 demonstrates the succession of activities that take place during the course of a fiscal year. The focal point of this model, its foundation, is the approved standard care or service HPM. **Each action within the system builds on the standard hours and all previous actions.** Because all of these subsequent functions build on the standard HPM, it's protected. The additional costs of fixed (indirect) and nonproductive salaries are added on in addition, so that hours budgeted to deliver a desired level of quality can be scheduled, staffed, and maintained throughout the fiscal year. The following example is a description of how the pattern is applied in one department.

Through careful collection, compilation, and validation of data logged during the past fiscal year, the manager of the perfusion technology department has documented the need for 6.0 hours of perfusionist time for each open heart surgery case. The budget committee approved the standard, 6.0 direct care hours for each of the projected 800 cases; and the resulting 3.0 FTEs were budgeted:

Perfusion Technology Resource Plan

$$800 \times 6.0 \div 2080 = 2.3 \text{ Direct FTEs}$$

$$2.3 \text{ Direct FTEs} + .5 \text{ Fixed FTEs}^* = 2.8 \text{ Productive FTEs}$$

$$2.3 \text{ Direct FTEs} \times 216^\dagger \div 2080 = 0.2 \text{ Nonproductive FTEs}$$

$$2.8 \text{ Prod. FTEs} + 0.2 \text{ Nonprod. FTEs} = 3.0 \text{ Total FTEs}$$

* Manager time split between managerial and technmical responsibilities   = .5 Fixed
† Average benefit hours

The approved figure of 3.0 was also used to develop a daily staffing pattern and in decisions about on-call planning and shift assignments. Due to the anticipated daily open heart surgery volume of 3.1 modalities (800 cases annually ÷ 260 operating days per year), the pattern showed a normal daily staffing compliment of 2 staff members (3.1 x 6.0 HPM = 18.6 hours ÷ 8-hour shifts = 2.3 staff members). The .3 FTE meant that hours for a third person were available for the one or two days per week, on the average, when there was a volume- or acuity-related need. On the occasions, later on, when the *actual* volume and acuity levels did not match budgeted expectations, the manager of this department reallocated staff, both in and out of the department,[8] in an ongoing effort to meet both quality and productivity goals. The ability of the department to meet the acuity and volume levels on a daily, shift-by-shift basis was monitored and documented concurrently, by each shift, and, as a result, became a retrospective record for future planning.

With this example in mind, review the **Resource (Cost) Management System** model on the next page, noting the importance and impact of the care or service HPM at each point in the cycle.

A Brief Look at Cost

So far, very little has been said about cost. Healthcare costing and pricing decisions are areas of study in themselves; however, they need to be mentioned here for perspective. One of the advantages of looking at the unit of service and our patient care or service HPM is to provide healthcare managers with pertinent information that will allow them to identify the actual costs of providing their service. Finding out the cost of many of our patient care or service modalities is relatively simple because labor generates most of the costs.

The importance of cost as a financial indicator is significant. Cost can be used as (1) baseline information for determining a profitable price; (2) an indicator of whether current costs are exceeding the current price; or, in a general sense, (3) criteria for determining the potential profitability of the department overall. All of these are planning functions. Managers who know how much labor time is consumed by the variety of services offered by their department will most certainly have the edge, not only to compete in the market but also to provide the kind of high quality in their services that will make a positive difference to both patients and employees. In addition, knowing the costs of department modalities leads to precise accounting of total departmental costs and paves the way toward accurate pricing of services.

The human resource department doesn't sell services, at least not in the usual sense; but it does have clients—the employees of the organization. By virtue of

---

[8] The concept of reallocation is easily stated here, but is an extremely sensitive, difficult issue to manage. It is the subject of the next section.

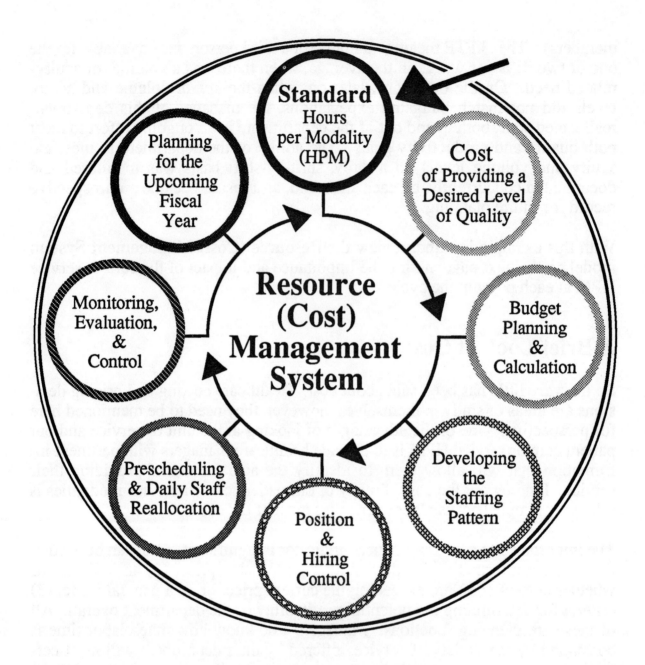

Resource (Cost) Management System

*All of the activities in the cycle build on the **standard** (large arrow). The standard represents the time, on the average, that will be available to employees for delivering their services at a predetermined and agreed on level of quality. Using the standard as baseline information for the remaining activities will protect it from being reduced by indirect patient care or services.*

Legend
Resource (Cost) Management System

Standard

The unit of service of the department. The following activities build on the approved (and budgeted) standard hours of care or service, on the average, planned to be delivered to a unit's patient or service population.

Cost

Determination of the cost of providing the desired hours per modality (HPM) based on skill level mix, the time it takes to provide care or the service at different levels of acuity, and average salary levels.

Budget Planning & Calculation

Once program planning and goals are formulated, approved HPM are used to determine labor requirements and costs. Direct FTEs are allocated based on HPM, and the fixed (indirect) and nonproductive hours build on top of the direct hours, so the hours for patient care or service delivery are more or less protected.

Developing the Staffing Pattern

A staffing pattern created using budgeted FTEs based on the average acuity and average volume facilitates adjustment for increased or decreased volume or acuity.

Position & Hiring Control

Once FTEs are budgeted and worked into a staffing pattern covering three shifts, there must be an organized, consistent commitment to hire only for available positions and within the approved salary range. Otherwise, it becomes impossible to meet budget targets without decreasing the HPM in our care or services.

Prescheduling & Daily Staff Reallocation

Staff hired into budgeted positions are prescheduled according to the annual staffing pattern. However, every day there are potential variances from the anticipated, budgeted average. The standard combined with daily acuity information gives managers the information they need to make appropriate staffing decisions.

Monitoring, Evaluation, & Control

Here the standard is used concurrently and retrospectively to assess the match of *classified* HPM to *budgeted* HPM to *actual* HPM provided to the patient. Concurrent use of the standard is useful because identified variances from the target can be adjusted immediately.

Planning for the Upcoming Fiscal Year

Analyzing classification data, volume, and financial data helps managers reassess their standard, adjust it, and prepare for the next budget cycle. Concurrent monitoring, when documented, generates excellent retrospective data for future planning decisions.

an approved budget, there is a predetermined workload expected of each employee. If workload increases, (1) people are worked overtime, (2) more dollars are spent than are allocated, and (3) the department exceeds its costs. In response to this the manager can (1) ignore it because it's justified, (2) force the workers to cut back on their overtime but maintain the workload, or (3) work with the employees (assuming they are working up to par) to identify how the workload can be reduced, simplified, reorganized, and, ultimately, reduced so they can complete their work within existing time constraints.

The outline below summarizes the benefits of identifying costs that are related to patient care and related service modalities.

Benefits of Cost Finding

- If cost exceeds price, a department cannot be considered to be financially independent or to be in a successful business situation.

- The use of costs as baseline information for costing care and services can lead to:
    - a change in the image of a department, from an "expense" to "profit maker."
    - a more equitable method of charging patients for services.

- Identified costs provide useful input for program planning activities, including documentation, justification, and evaluation. Validated information gives credible support to decision making.

- When the cost of providing a service is known, institutions are in a better position for negotiation agreements with PPOs, HMOs, and other third party payers.

*Making resources productive
is the specific job of
management,
as distinct from other
jobs of the "manager":
entrepreneurship and
administration.
It is only **managers** — not
nature or laws of economics
or governments — that
make resources productive.*

Peter Drucker
<u>MANAGING IN TURBULENT TIMES</u>

Section 3

Reallocating Employees to Meet Variable Demand

Productivity is a topic people talk about often, but being able to walk the talk becomes another matter. I promised this workbook would be a hands-on approach to management, and this section begins the activity. First some clarifications and assumptions:

Assumptions

- Projected volume of modalities (activity level) has been targeted and agreed on;

- A system of logging and identifying labor consumption by modality is in use;

- Acuity targets (care or service HPM) have been
    - logged and justified
    - budgeted and approved; and

- Staffing pattern has been set and staff is routinely prescheduled accordingly.

To some extent, this workbook picks up where **Healthcare Staffing & Budgeting: Practical Management Tools** leaves off. Considering the above assumptions, employees have already been prescheduled and assigned according to the annual staffing pattern several weeks before the actual time period covered. The schedules are not referred to again until each day arrives, and determinations are made regarding adjustments for *actual* acuity or volume (which may be different from what was anticipated and formally projected). Actual acuity and volume demands that have varied from projections are usually met through reallocation of staff working hours.

Daily Staffing Decisions

When a department is committed to a volume-based budget, it means that the manager has (1) identified the average hours of care, or service, that will be needed, (2) calculated a budget using that average; and (3) planned to use the approved HPM as a guide to staff the department on a daily basis. Although it is true that budgets are not always approved for the original desired HPM, assume for this section that that is the case. A later section on work simplification is devoted to the subject of what to do when required hours are more than budgeted hours.

If staffing decisions were based only on the budgeted HPM, without regard for actual acuity requirements, daily staffing would be simple. The graph below demonstrates how many hours of staff time would be provided to a department approved for 0.5 HPM (30 minutes). Formula: ([Modality Volume] x [.5 HPM]).

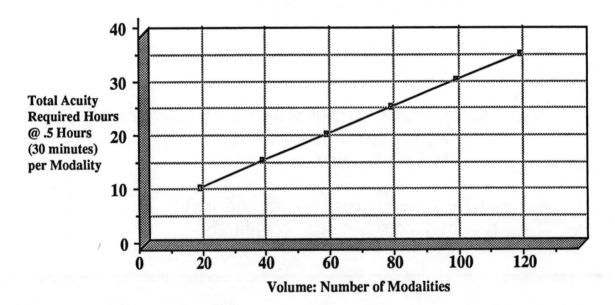

However, that's only part of the picture. The opposite page illustrates one of the most important concepts in this workbook, capsulizing the essence of the daily staffing decision. All three targets must be considered each time a staff allocation

Budgeted

Budgeted HPM:

A department's productivity target. Based on the expected average acuity or patient care hours required per modality. Used in conjunction with projected modalities to calculate the number of personnel (FTEs) needed for the upcoming fiscal year.

Targets:
Patient Care & Related Services

Classified HPM:

An outcome of the classification system. Time values are assigned to department modalities to enable average hours required by actual modalities to be accumulated and averaged. When economically feasible, the annual average becomes the budgeted HPM; and, if not, work needs to be done to simplify and streamline the workload. Classified HPM change with the profile of patient acuity needs and generate a new "quality target" with each change.

Classified

Actual HPM:

The actual direct care hours delivered, per modality, on the average. After modalities are classified, attempts are made to alter the number of staff members scheduled for that shift in an effort to match the classified hours needed. At the same time the budget must also be considered. Actual HPM are used in conjunction with classified and budgeted HPMs to ascertain the variances among what was budgeted, what was really needed (classified), and what was actually provided.

Actual

decision is made. Even though the *budgeted* .5 HPM is based on budgeted expectation of staffing needs, the *classified* HPM required by the current patients or clients requesting services may differ from expectation and, therefore, must be re-addressed. *Actual* assigned and provided staff generate a third HPM target. All three must be reviewed and responded to every shift, every day of the year.

- **Budgeted HPM**   This figure is already reflected in prescheduling but should be reviewed in retrospect to staffing and reallocation decisions and used for future planning purposes.

- **Classified HPM**   This is the end result of classifying modalities into categories with predetermined time values assigned to them. It is calculated by adding up all the individual time values of the modalities ordered and dividing by the number of modalities.

- **Actual HPM**   This is actual staff provided per modality. If five emergency department employees each work a total of 40 hours with each of 20 patient visits, each patient receives an average of 2 hours per modality.

Using Classification Information for Adjusting Daily Staffing Plans

As stated earlier, managers can plan for the average volume and the average acuity required HPM but never really know, until a particular day arrives, what will be needed. The **Staffing Report**, Form 3.1, is a tool for daily decision making that also can be used as a retrospective data record for future planning and budgeting. There are standard time values for each modality.[9] As shown in the example on the top of the next page, modality #1 requires 0.25 hours (15 minutes) on the average; modality #2, 0.5 hours (30 minutes) on the average, and so on.

---

[9] Standard time values for specific modalities can be preprinted on the form after they are defined and approved. Unless an official (usually administrative) decision is made to alter that figure, the care hours for a given modality or service do not change (e.g., an electrocardiogram [ECG] in a particular department always takes 25 minutes ± 5 minutes). If, however, the age of the patient population changes over time, and the impact is a *trend* toward 40-minute ECGs, then it's time to collect data to see if an increase in the standard HPM is indicated...and affordable.

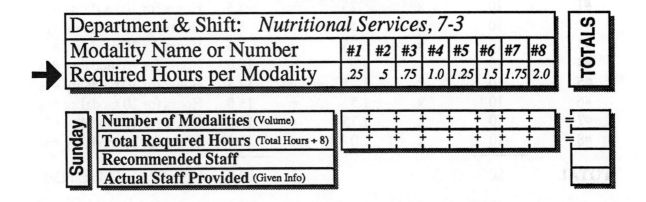

Before the start of the shift the manager or person responsible for allocating staff should collect both volume and acuity data. In the example below, the department offers 8 different modalities and each requires varying amounts of time from staff members. Remember, the assumption is that these time values have been analyzed and validated. In this case, 10 of each of the modalities (a total of 80) have been ordered.

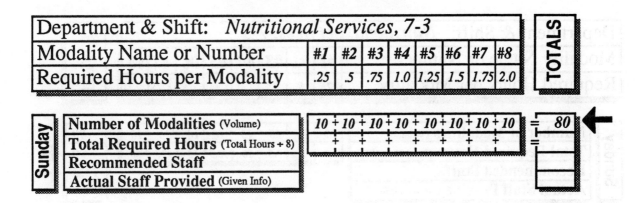

So far, I have not addressed the budget or the number of prescheduled staff because the objective, at this point, is to identify required hours of care (or services) for the actual modalities ordered. This is accomplished by accumulating total hours required for each modality. The table at the top of the next page demonstrates the step-by step process in detail; however, in practice, it takes only a few minutes daily to do the calculations.

Modality	Volume		HPM		Cumulative Required Hours	
#1	10	x	.25	=	2.5	Hours for 10 modality #1s
#2	10	x	.5	=	5.0	Hours for 10 modality #2s
#3	10	x	.75	=	7.5	Hours for 10 modality #3s
#4	10	x	1.0	=	10.0	Hours for 10 modality #4s
#5	10	x	1.25	=	12.5	Hours for 10 modality #5s
#6	10	x	1.5	=	15.0	Hours for 10 modality #6s
#7	10	x	1.75	=	17.5	Hours for 10 modality #7s
#8	10	x	2.0	=	20.0	Hours for 10 modality #8s
TOTAL	**80**				**90.0**	**Hours for all Modalities**

Next, if each staff member works an 8-hour shift, that means there should be 11 staff members on duty (90 Required Hours ÷ 8-hour shifts = 11.2[10]) during the time the modalities need to be delivered. If the department is open for only one shift, all 11 would be on at the same time. If it was open for two shifts, the staff would be split (by a predetermined percentage) between the two shifts. For simplicity in the example, assume it is a one-shift department.

Staffing Report

Department & Shift: *Nutritional Services, 7-3*									TOTALS
Modality Name or Number	#1	#2	#3	#4	#5	#6	#7	#8	
Required Hours per Modality	.25	.5	.75	1.0	1.25	1.5	1.75	2.0	

Sunday										
Number of Modalities (Volume)	10	10	10	10	10	10	10	10	=	80
Total Required Hours (Total Hrs ÷ 8)	2.5	5	7.5	10	12.5	15	17.5	20	=	90 ←
Recommended Staff										11.2 ←
Actual Staff Provided (Given Info)										

If the approved and budgeted HPM were 1.0 and we prescheduled for that target, there would already have been 10 staff members (80 modalities x 1.0 Budgeted

---

[10] The .25 can be ignored or considered. It just gives the manager information that a fraction more than 11 staff members is needed. The manager could assign 2 extra staff hours, preferably not at overtime rate, to be precise. I prefer to leave it to manager judgment based on his or her particular situation, staff mix, skill levels of staff members assigned, etc. These numbers are indicators—to help managers make decisions—not answers.

HPM ÷ 8-hour shifts[11] = 10 staff) assigned that day. However, the classified (or actual acuity required) hours were higher than the budget target (90 accumulated hours ÷ 80 modalities = 1.1 HPM). In this case, there would be a need to add 10 hours of staff time to the prescheduled staff assignment. On another day with 90 modalities that have lower than projected acuities, there may be justification, according to actual acuity required hours, to reduce staffing.

Thus, volume isn't the bottom line even in a volume-based budget system. Acuity must also be taken into consideration. Some healthcare organizations are staffed only according to volume because it's easier to control. Managers are more likely to get into trouble adjusting for daily acuity variations because the natural tendency is to adjust only in one direction...up. Some have no problem adding staff when acuities are high; others develop a paralysis when it comes to decreasing. If you have budgeted for your average acuity, say 1.0 HPM, that means that sometimes you'll need less, sometimes more, sometimes that exact amount. Thus, if you adjust honestly for acuity, both up and down, over the long range you should come out on target. On the other hand, some managers prefer to staff just to the budget target (1.0 in this case) and adjust only for volume, as shown in the last segment of the demonstration example, above (arrow). It's a manager's choice; but, in this case, that decision would result in an extra hour of work during the shift for each of the 10 employees on duty.

Staffing Report

Department & Shift: *Nutritional Services, 7-3*									TOTALS
Modality Name or Number	#1	#2	#3	#4	#5	#6	#7	#8	
Required Hours per Modality	.25	.5	.75	1.0	1.25	1.5	1.75	2.0	

Sunday		#1	#2	#3	#4	#5	#6	#7	#8	TOTALS
	Number of Modalities (Volume)	10	+10	+10	+10	+10	+10	+10	+10	= 80
	Total Required Hours (Total Hrs ÷ 8)	2.5	+5	+7.5	+10	+12.5	+15	+17.5	+20	= 90
	Recommended Staff									11.2
	Actual Staff Provided (Given Info)									10 ←

The Actual Staff Provided (above) is documentation of whatever the manager decided to staff. It may or may not match the Recommended Staff. Remember that this is a guide for the manager, not an answer. In the final analysis managers must

---

[11] Shift variations of any length can be used. If the staff members in this department worked 10-hour shifts, then 8 staff (80 ÷ 10 = 8) would have been assigned.

rely on a combination of their experience and their professional judgment, in addition to this information, to make what they believe to be the best decision.

There is no reference to the budgeted HPM (that will come later), but let's make some suppositions for the purpose of discussion. Assume for a moment that (1) the budgeted HPM is 1.0 hours, (2) the department is open for only one shift, and (3) 12 staff members were actually on duty providing care.

Budgeted HPM	Classified HPM	Actual HPM
10 staff x 8 hours = 80 staff hours 80 hrs ÷ 80 modalities = 1.0 HPM	Recommended Staff = 90 staff hours 90 hrs ÷ 80 modalities = 1.1 HPM	12 staff x 8 hours = 96 staff hours 96 hrs ÷ 80 modalities = 1.2 HPM

The classification information indicates that more hours are needed to take care of the current modality workload than were anticipated at the time the budget was calculated. The .1 hour (6 minutes) variance (1.1 HPM - 1.0 HPM) for the total 90 modalities means an additional 9 staff hours (.1 x 90) for the shift. If the department were staffed for 1.2 HPM, .1 HPM *more* than needed, there would be an unjustified variance (0.1 from what was needed and .2 from what was budgeted). Six minutes may not seem like a large variance, and it's not. But it's a lot easier to manage 6-minute variances than it is to manage being over target 6 FTEs. That will be addressed more completely in the next section.

This procedure is repeated each shift of every day, using the same process. Although it is time consuming to teach, calculating it takes only about a minute. The purpose of the **Staffing Report** is to document recommended staffing according to acuity requirements. It gives the manager concurrent and retrospective data to help him or her arrive at the best decision. However, it cannot replace the necessary managerial judgment that is required to compile and analyze all variables for staffing decisions. The manager may opt, for a variety of reasons, to vary from suggested recommended staffing.

The remainder of the form is shown on the next two pages as both a completed example and a blank, camera-ready version for immediate use.

Staffing Report

Department & Shift: *Nutritional Services, 7-3*									
Modality Name or Number	*#1*	*#2*	*#3*	*#4*	*#5*	*#6*	*#7*	*#8*	**TOTALS**
Required Hours per Modality	.25	.5	.75	1.0	1.25	1.5	1.75	2.0	

Sunday

	#1	#2	#3	#4	#5	#6	#7	#8	TOTALS
Number of Modalities (Volume)	10 +	10 +	10 +	10 +	10 +	10 +	10 +	10	= 80
Total Required Hours (Total Hrs ÷ 8)	2.5 +	5 +	7.5 +	10 +	12.5 +	15 +	17.5 +	20	= 90
Recommended Staff									11.2
Actual Staff Provided (Given Info)									10

Monday

	#1	#2	#3	#4	#5	#6	#7	#8	TOTALS
Number of Modalities (Volume)	4 +	8 +	8 +	10 +	12 +	20 +	24 +	30	= 116
Total Required Hours (Total Hrs ÷ 8)	1 +	4 +	6 +	10 +	15 +	30 +	42 +	60	= 168
Recommended Staff									21
Actual Staff Provided (Given Info)									14

Tuesday

	#1	#2	#3	#4	#5	#6	#7	#8	TOTALS
Number of Modalities (Volume)	32 +	30 +	24 +	20 +	12 +	10 +	8 +	8	= 144
Total Required Hours (Total Hrs ÷ 8)	8 +	15 +	18 +	20 +	15 +	15 +	14 +	16	= 121
Recommended Staff									15.1
Actual Staff Provided (Given Info)									18

Wednesday

	#1	#2	#3	#4	#5	#6	#7	#8	TOTALS
Number of Modalities (Volume)	20 +	20 +	20 +	20 +	20 +	20 +	20 +	20	= 160
Total Required Hours (Total Hrs ÷ 8)	5 +	10 +	15 +	20 +	25 +	30 +	35 +	40	= 180
Recommended Staff									22.5
Actual Staff Provided (Given Info)									20

Thursday

	#1	#2	#3	#4	#5	#6	#7	#8	TOTALS
Number of Modalities (Volume)	0 +	0 +	0 +	0 +	0 +	40 +	40 +	40	= 120
Total Required Hours (Total Hrs ÷ 8)	0 +	0 +	0 +	0 +	0 +	60 +	70 +	80	= 210
Recommended Staff									26.2
Actual Staff Provided (Given Info)									15

Friday

	#1	#2	#3	#4	#5	#6	#7	#8	TOTALS
Number of Modalities (Volume)	+	+	+	+	+	+	+		=
Total Required Hours (Total Hrs ÷ 8)	+	+	+	+	+	+	+		=
Recommended Staff									
Actual Staff Provided (Given Info)									

Saturday

	#1	#2	#3	#4	#5	#6	#7	#8	TOTALS
Number of Modalities (Volume)	+	+	+	+	+	+	+		=
Total Required Hours (Total Hrs ÷ 8)	+	+	+	+	+	+	+		=
Recommended Staff									
Actual Staff Provided (Given Info)									

Form 3.1-Example

Staffing Report

Department & Shift:									TOTALS
Modality Name or Number									
Required Hours per Modality									

Sunday

	+	+	+	+	+	+	+	=
Number of Modalities (Volume)								
Total Required Hours (Total Hrs ÷ 8)	+	+	+	+	+	+	+	=
Recommended Staff								
Actual Staff Provided (Given Info)								

Monday

	+	+	+	+	+	+	+	=
Number of Modalities (Volume)								
Total Required Hours (Total Hrs ÷ 8)	+	+	+	+	+	+	+	=
Recommended Staff								
Actual Staff Provided (Given Info)								

Tuesday

	+	+	+	+	+	+	+	=
Number of Modalities (Volume)								
Total Required Hours (Total Hrs ÷ 8)	+	+	+	+	+	+	+	=
Recommended Staff								
Actual Staff Provided (Given Info)								

Wednesday

	+	+	+	+	+	+	+	=
Number of Modalities (Volume)								
Total Required Hours (Total Hrs ÷ 8)	+	+	+	+	+	+	+	=
Recommended Staff								
Actual Staff Provided (Given Info)								

Thursday

	+	+	+	+	+	+	+	=
Number of Modalities (Volume)								
Total Required Hours (Total Hrs ÷ 8)	+	+	+	+	+	+	+	=
Recommended Staff								
Actual Staff Provided (Given Info)								

Friday

	+	+	+	+	+	+	+	=
Number of Modalities (Volume)								
Total Required Hours (Total Hrs ÷ 8)	+	+	+	+	+	+	+	=
Recommended Staff								
Actual Staff Provided (Given Info)								

Saturday

	+	+	+	+	+	+	+	=
Number of Modalities (Volume)								
Total Required Hours (Total Hrs ÷ 8)	+	+	+	+	+	+	+	=
Recommended Staff								
Actual Staff Provided (Given Info)								

How to Reallocate Staff

I've talked a lot about reallocating—both adding and reducing—staff. It's an easy concept to talk about, but doing it can be difficult and time consuming (not to mention life threatening) if you don't plan ahead and have good systems in place.

Have you heard these statements?: "All you care about is numbers"..."I have a personal life too"..."the staffing is *dangerous*"..."it's not my turn to float."

Day-to-day staffing decisions regarding allocations of staff follow the same guidelines that were set up at the time budgets were planned. The manager

All managers have days when they wish they could do this with their staff members.

who has reviewed annual staffing goals and objectives with his or her staff should have no problem reviewing daily reallocations that meet those objectives. Here, as always, the more information that staff members have and the more they understand the goals they are working toward have not sacrificed quality, the better they will be able to comply with the outcomes. To maximize the benefit from the data base as well as managerial judgment, the manager generally looks at the following four areas when making daily staffing decisions:

- **Classification information** – indicator of acuity and recommended staffing level

- **Volume** – number of modalities ordered, or expected, during the shift

- **Staff mix** – ratio or percentage of different skill levels prescheduled

- **Individual staff members' skill level** – years of experience and current ability to function at their designated capacity (i.e., a new graduate on his or her first day out of orientation may not produce as abundantly as a worker with three years' experience)

Deciding to adjust staffing is one thing; making it happen, without mutiny, is another. Moving staff members around is not just an exercise in accounting for staff hours on a piece of paper. As managers we are rearranging people's lives, sometimes floating them to strange units, and maybe even laying them off. We must plan and consider their input and needs carefully. On the following page are some tips for reallocating staff successfully.

Life-Saving Reallocation Tips

- *Learn the art of negotiation...fast!*

- *Make it possible for your staff members to get involved in decisions about their destiny:*

  - *If you're facing a downsizing (reduction in staff), find out if they'd rather be laid off or cross-trained to another department; if they'd rather take a day off without pay or be sent home with vacation pay; if they'd rather work an 11-7 shift than float.*

  - *If you're facing a surge in volume, find out if they'd prefer to work overtime rather than bring in agency assistance; if they'd rather work a day off or a double, etc.*

  Managers may not be able to change what has to be done, but they certainly can give their employees choices about the most palatable way to do something they don't want to do.

- *Investigate and set up systems for voluntary increase and decrease of staff hours.*

- *Hire less staff to a department's permanent staff and allocate more budgeted positions to per diem staff or even a float pool.*

• *Appreciate part-time staff, both those who may work regularly (e.g., three days per week) and those who work sporadically (e.g., one day per month).*

• *Let staff get involved with management in planning staffing systems and policies. It will ensure fairness, consistency, understanding, and employee support.*

• *Tell potential employees the truth about staffing and reallocation policies before they are hired so they don't feel betrayed (not to mention hostile) after they come to work in your department.*

• *Plan carefully when you do float staff. Do it gently, thoughtfully, and with respect for the worker who may be terrified of unfamiliar assignments, surroundings, and coworkers.*

Section 4

Monitoring, Evaluation, & Control

Usually, organizational management reports of budgetary performance are not available for managers until well past the time when significant changes can be made to improve performance. Feedforward monitoring and control means that the manager can control, in advance and concurrently, both short- and long-range outcomes of performance. We've already started the process in the early sections in the workbook. On a daily basis, actual volume and acuity requirements can be reviewed, staff can be reallocated accordingly, and an evaluation can be made by comparing actual performance to the predetermined quality and productivity standards. If actual staffing doesn't match the target, then there is still time to make changes and improve quality, before the situation gets out of control.

The purpose of productivity monitoring and evaluation is not just to red flag a situation that is out of control. On the contrary, its focus is positive; it is designed to assist managers in being proactive about maintaining departmental personnel hours and expenses within predetermined constraints. The theory is that, if a department maintains its productivity standards, i.e., quality and cost effectiveness throughout the fiscal year, it will automatically be *on target annually*. This section is about how to make that theory a reality.

Why is being *on target* important? Institutional survival is one reason, and manager accountability is another, now that many managers' merit increases depend on performance in this area. Both of these are very serious factors; but an even more important consideration is that in our current healthcare system there are a finite number of direct and indirect care hours available for patients. We are, in effect, rationing healthcare based on economics. For example, the manager of a patient care department has budgeted 1.0 hours of care for the upcoming fiscal year's projected modalities. In the department a variety of modalities are offered that range in time value from 30 minutes to 1.5 hours. Although planning was based on an average of 1.0 HPM, on a given day an average of the ordered modalities may be as low as .5 HPM or as high as 1.5 HPM. To use budgeted labor resources to the best advantage, the manager needs to be able to adjust staffing to the needs of those varied occasions while he or she tracks how this is affecting budgetary performance and the financial goals of the organization.

Comparing Actual Performance to Classified Need

On any given day or shift a manager can identify the acuity needs, in hours, of the patients in need of care or the departments in need of services, if the classification system has time values attached to either activities or classification levels, as in the example below. I will review two different productivity and quality monitoring tools. In the first one classification levels will be used; in the second one time values will be assigned to actual modalities. The first is the most effective tool for departments that don't have specific or time-weighted modalities, or that are still in the process of defining time values and want to collect information. In addition, some progressive professionally staffed departments are beginning to look at charging by professional time consumed; and the first method, using the **Productivity & Acuity Report**, Form 4.1, would be most appropriate for that kind of monitoring.

To the right, and at the top of the next page, is a one-day cut from **Productivity & Acuity Report**, Form 4.1. To keep things simple, assume that the staff of the department does a variety of modalities; but all of the modalities take either 0.5, 1.0, or 1.5 hours to complete. The department is operational for two shifts, 7 days per week. On this day, 64 modalities are

Identifying classified (actual acuity required) care or service hours

CLASS LEVEL	STANDARD HRS PER MODALITY	x	VOLUME	=	ACUITY REQUIRED HOURS
I	.5	x	20	=	10
II	1.0	x	24	=	24
III	1.5	x	20	=	30
Totals			64	=	64

scheduled. It is expected that 20 will require 0.5 hours; 24, 1.0 hours; 20, 1.5 hours, for a total of 64 hours. Knowing this information, the manager will try to staff 64 hours (8 employees working 8-hour shifts) between the two shifts. After the classification process, staffing assignments will be made and compared to budget targets to assess productivity and budget performance (top of next page). Keep in mind, this example is a purely utopian situation where the classified and acuity required hours (1.0 HPM) matched the preset budget expectation (1.0 HPM) and then staff were scheduled according to that need (1.0 HPM).[12] On each

---

[12] The chance of this actually occurring is rare; however, it serves as a goal to the manager trying to coordinate and bring together as tightly as possible three targets (budgeted, classified, and actual) to achieve maximal quality and productivity.

Comparing volume-adjusted budgeted care or service hours to actual provided hours

SHIFT	BUDGETED HPM (Standard)	x	VOLUME	=	TOTAL HRS PER BUDGET	ACTUAL HOURS = Staff x 8	VARIANCE ( ) = Under Target
7-3	1.0	x	40	=	40	40	0
3-11	1.0	x	24	=	24	24	0
11-7	1.0	x	0	=	0	0	0
Totals	1.0		64		64	64	0

shift there is a zero variance from the budget target. If the classified hours indicated a total requirement of 80 hours and the manager staffed to meet that need, then there would be a positive variance of 16 hours, indicating that the department is 16 hours over budget target. However, this is justified by the acuity requirements of the services being delivered that day.

Comparing Actual Performance to Budgeted Expectations

A second example (below) using the same acuity classification information as the previous example, shows a different reaction by the manager. Classifications indicate a need for a total of 64 staff hours between the two shifts, and the manager allocated 32 hours on days (7-3) and 32 hours on evenings (3-11). The variance for the whole day was on target; but it looks like the department was overstaffed on the 7-3 shift and understaffed on the 3-11 shift. There is no way for us to know what happened from these data, but the manager knows and sometimes he or she makes notes in the margins about what happened to cause the variances. As

Comparing volume-adjusted budgeted care or service hours to actual provided hours

SHIFT	BUDGETED HPM (Standard)	x	VOLUME	=	TOTAL HRS PER BUDGET	ACTUAL HOURS = Staff x 8	VARIANCE ( ) = Under Target
7-3	1.0	x	32	=	32	40	8
3-11	1.0	x	32	=	32	24	(8)
11-7	1.0	x	0	=	0	0	0
Totals	1.0		64		64	64	0

examples, absences, new staff, extraordinary patient events, new physician expectations, and demands from administration can impact on staffing needs. If (1) JCAHO is coming and the halls need extra cleaning, or (2) a patient needs more than the "allotted" time for a modality, that's probably going to impact on staffing. The short-range significance is over-target variances. The long-range significance comes with planning for these occasions with contingency plans and decreases in staffing when acuity permits.

In the final example (right) the classification information changes. There are still 64 modalities expected, but they are low-acuity modalities accumulating a need for only 44 hours of staff time. Looking at the actual staffing and budget situation above, a staffing-to-budget target for 1.0 HPM with a zero variance to budget is

Identifying classified (actual acuity required) care or service hours

CLASS LEVEL	STANDARD HRS PER MODALITY	x	VOLUME	=	ACUITY REQUIRED HOURS
I	.5	x	40	=	20
II	1.0	x	24	=	24
III	1.5	x	0	=	0
Totals			64	=	44

Comparing volume-adjusted budgeted care or service hours to actual provided hours

SHIFT	BUDGETED HPM (Standard)	x	VOLUME	=	TOTAL HRS PER BUDGET	ACTUAL HOURS = Staff x 8	VARIANCE ( ) = Under Target
7-3	1.0	x	64	=	64	64	0
3-11	1.0	x	0	=	0	8	8
11-7	1.0	x	0	=	0	0	0
Totals	1.0		64		64	72	8

shown, but from the acuity information we can see that the department had 20 hours more than actually needed. The manager should have tried to reallocate someone from the 7-3 shift. Sometimes, the 8 hours over target on the 3-11 shift may be unavoidable if someone must be available for *unscheduled* requests; but, whenever this is the case, you should be prepared to give this person some work that needs to be done so this is not down time.[13] Remember, it's not just the money that's lost; it's time for patient care or related services that's lost—time that may not be able to be reclaimed.

---

[13] Reference Section 6 for ideas on how to make good use of what's known as "down time." It doesn't have to be unproductive.

Not everyone works in a department with all prescheduled modalities and a full staffing compliment to increase and decrease at will. In fact, most healthcare managers probably don't work with either of those situations; and even when they do plan, they do so with the knowledge that it will probably change. The constant variable is the commitment to quality service delivery; and even if we have little control over those variables, documenting this information will still help managers do their job better. It gives them a methodology to assess, evaluate, and take responsible action toward the quality and productivity goals of the unit, confidently and quickly. It takes 3 minutes daily (5 for those who are calculator dependent) to complete. This tool can give managers control and authority over an activity that has long been an uncontrollable and uncomfortable responsibility. An example and blank version of **Productivity & Acuity Report**, Form 4.1 are displayed on pages 55 and 56.

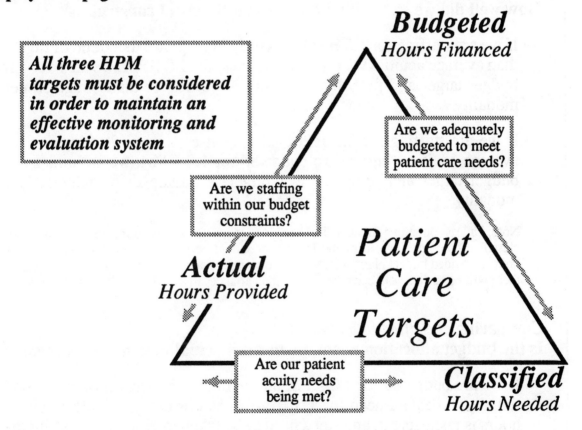

In summary, for about 3 minutes a day, a department manager can look at (1) acuity classified, (2) budgeted, and (3) actual HPM, and make an assessment of overall department performance as it relates to both quality and productivity. In addition, some managers keep a running total of their accumulated *actual to budget* daily balances and know, on any day, any shift during the fiscal year, how close they are to the annual budget target. No more surprises when the financials are published!

Comparing *actual* to *classified*
How well were patient acuity needs being met?

- If we are staffing for 1.0 HPM but our acuity ratings indicate the patients require 1.5 HPM, we are not (at least on paper) staffing sufficiently to meet identified patient care or related services needs.

- If we are staffing for 1.0 HPM but our acuity ratings indicate the patients require 0.5 HPM, we are staffing for more hours than are needed to meet identified patient care or related services requirements.

Comparing *actual* to *budgeted*
How well did we stay within budget and financial constraints?

- If we are staffing for 1.5 HPM (possibly in response to a trend of higher than average acuities) but we are budgeted for 1.0 HPM, we are over our budget target and probably spending more dollars than budgeted per modality.

- If we are staffing for 0.5 HPM (in response to a trend of lower than average acuities) but we are budgeted for 1.0 HPM, we are under our budget target and probably spending less dollars than budgeted per modality.

Note: Unless something dramatic has happened to change a long-range trend, the average classified hours needed during the fiscal year should be about the same as the budgeted hours (provided budget planning was based on average acuity). However, on a daily basis, there will be variances in accordance with the variances in actual acuity required hours.

Comparing *classified* to *budgeted*
Is the budget allocation adequate to meet actual patient care needs?

- If we are budgeted for 1.0 HPM and validated classification data continually indicate a need for 1.5 HPM, then our budgeted allocation of hours is insufficient; and steps need to be taken to either increase budgeted HPM or to simplify or streamline the workload. (Note: This activity will be discussed in Section 6.)

- If we are budgeted for 1.0 HPM and validated classification data over the long range indicate a need for only 0.5 HPM, then our budgeted HPM can be reduced so that hours can be reallocated where needed.

Productivity & Acuity Report

Unit: _____
Period Beginning: _____

Sunday

Identifying classified (actual acuity required) care or service hours						Comparing volume-adjusted budgeted care or service hours to actual provided hours							
CLASS LEVEL	STANDARD HRS PER MODALITY	x	VOLUME	=	ACUITY REQUIRED HOURS	SHIFT	BUDGETED HPM (Standard)	x	VOLUME	=	TOTAL HRS PER BUDGET	ACTUAL HOURS = Staff x 8	VARIANCE ( ) = Under Target
I	.5	x	20	=	10	7-3	1.0	x	40	=	40	40	0
II	1.0	x	24	=	24	3-11	1.0	x	24	=	24	24	0
III	1.5	x	20	=	30	11-7	1.0	x	0	=	0	0	0
Totals			64	=	64	Totals	1.0		64		64	64	0

Monday

CLASS LEVEL	STANDARD HRS PER MODALITY	x	VOLUME	=	ACUITY REQUIRED HOURS	SHIFT	BUDGETED HPM (Standard)	x	VOLUME	=	TOTAL HRS PER BUDGET	ACTUAL HOURS = Staff x 8	VARIANCE ( ) = Under Target
I	.5	x	20	=	10	7-3	1.0	x	32	=	32	40	8
II	1.0	x	24	=	24	3-11	1.0	x	32	=	32	24	(8)
III	1.5	x	20	=	30	11-7	1.0	x	0	=	0	0	0
Totals			64	=	64	Totals	1.0		64		64	64	0

Tuesday

CLASS LEVEL	STANDARD HRS PER MODALITY	x	VOLUME	=	ACUITY REQUIRED HOURS	SHIFT	BUDGETED HPM (Standard)	x	VOLUME	=	TOTAL HRS PER BUDGET	ACTUAL HOURS = Staff x 8	VARIANCE ( ) = Under Target
I	.5	x	40	=	20	7-3	1.0	x	64	=	64	64	0
II	1.0	x	24	=	24	3-11	1.0	x	0	=	0	8	8
III	1.5	x	0	=	0	11-7	1.0	x	0	=	0	0	0
Totals			64	=	44	Totals	1.0		64		64	72	8

*The **Cumulative Balance** shows the department manager, on any shift, day, or week of the fiscal year, how actual performance compares to the budgeted target. An accumulated, running total of the variances show that 8 hours have accumulated in the "bank." This tells the department manager (1) where the department stands with regard to the budgeted target and (2) that the department has a current cushion of 8 hours. The department manager may use those hours for policy writing or planning, or just hold on to them for the next time acuities are higher than the expected norm. Knowing the cumulative balance gives managers choices and also provides a quick indication of the overall picture.[14]*

Variances aren't good or bad; they are indicators. The larger the variance, the more important it is for a manager to investigate and understand what is causing the variance.

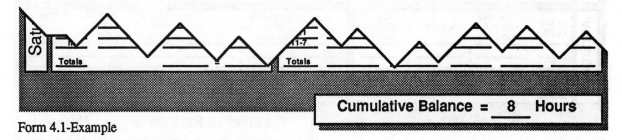

Cumulative Balance = 8 Hours

Form 4.1-Example

---

[14] One manager, when asked if she was interested in putting this collection of data on computer, said it would take her longer to walk to the computer and punch it in than it would take her to calculate it.

Productivity & Acuity Report

Unit: _____
Period Beginning: _____

Identifying classified (actual acuity required) care or service hours	Comparing volume-adjusted budgeted care or service hours to actual provided hours

Sunday

CLASS LEVEL	STANDARD HRS PER MODALITY	x	VOLUME	=	ACUITY REQUIRED HOURS
I		x		=	
II		x		=	
III		x		=	
Totals				=	

SHIFT	BUDGETED HPM (Standard)	x	VOLUME	=	TOTAL HRS PER BUDGET	ACTUAL HOURS = Staff x 8	VARIANCE ( ) = Under Target
7-3		x		=			
3-11		x		=			
11-7		x		=			
Totals							

Monday

CLASS LEVEL	STANDARD HRS PER MODALITY	x	VOLUME	=	ACUITY REQUIRED HOURS
I		x		=	
II		x		=	
III		x		=	
Totals				=	

SHIFT	BUDGETED HPM (Standard)	x	VOLUME	=	TOTAL HRS PER BUDGET	ACTUAL HOURS = Staff x 8	VARIANCE ( ) = Under Target
7-3		x		=			
3-11		x		=			
11-7		x		=			
Totals							

Tuesday

CLASS LEVEL	STANDARD HRS PER MODALITY	x	VOLUME	=	ACUITY REQUIRED HOURS
I		x		=	
II		x		=	
III		x		=	
Totals				=	

SHIFT	BUDGETED HPM (Standard)	x	VOLUME	=	TOTAL HRS PER BUDGET	ACTUAL HOURS = Staff x 8	VARIANCE ( ) = Under Target
7-3		x		=			
3-11		x		=			
11-7		x		=			
Totals							

Wednesday

CLASS LEVEL	STANDARD HRS PER MODALITY	x	VOLUME	=	ACUITY REQUIRED HOURS
I		x		=	
II		x		=	
III		x		=	
Totals				=	

SHIFT	BUDGETED HPM (Standard)	x	VOLUME	=	TOTAL HRS PER BUDGET	ACTUAL HOURS = Staff x 8	VARIANCE ( ) = Under Target
7-3		x		=			
3-11		x		=			
11-7		x		=			
Totals							

Thursday

CLASS LEVEL	STANDARD HRS PER MODALITY	x	VOLUME	=	ACUITY REQUIRED HOURS
I		x		=	
II		x		=	
III		x		=	
Totals				=	

SHIFT	BUDGETED HPM (Standard)	x	VOLUME	=	TOTAL HRS PER BUDGET	ACTUAL HOURS = Staff x 8	VARIANCE ( ) = Under Target
7-3		x		=			
3-11		x		=			
11-7		x		=			
Totals							

Friday

CLASS LEVEL	STANDARD HRS PER MODALITY	x	VOLUME	=	ACUITY REQUIRED HOURS
I		x		=	
II		x		=	
III		x		=	
Totals				=	

SHIFT	BUDGETED HPM (Standard)	x	VOLUME	=	TOTAL HRS PER BUDGET	ACTUAL HOURS = Staff x 8	VARIANCE ( ) = Under Target
7-3		x		=			
3-11		x		=			
11-7		x		=			
Totals							

Saturday

CLASS LEVEL	STANDARD HRS PER MODALITY	x	VOLUME	=	ACUITY REQUIRED HOURS
I		x		=	
II		x		=	
III		x		=	
Totals				=	

SHIFT	BUDGETED HPM (Standard)	x	VOLUME	=	TOTAL HRS PER BUDGET	ACTUAL HOURS = Staff x 8	VARIANCE ( ) = Under Target
7-3		x		=			
3-11		x		=			
11-7		x		=			
Totals							

Cumulative Balance = _____ Hours

Form 4.1

Productivity Worksheets

When data start to accumulate and become cumbersome to handle and analyze, it's time to collect the information and organize it into a manageable and meaningful report. In this section are several different formats for organizing quality and productivity information for your own use, or to share with others. They all have one common feature; that is they provide a way for the manager to compare budgeted, classified, and actual hours on a total and per modality basis.

The **Productivity & Acuity Report**, Form 4.1, and the other reports following cover a two-week period, to coincide with biweekly payroll periods. However, each format can be adapted for any time period from a week, to biweekly pay periods, to months, to a fiscal year. All the required information for the forms should be available to managers; however, if it's not, here are some places where you can find your management information:

Where to Find Productivity Information

A. Volume of Modalities
- accumulated tally of the actual volume of services completed
- business office: total modality charges = total delivered modalities
- management financial reports (usually several weeks later)

B. Total Hours Required as per Budget
- approved and budgeted HPM multiplied by the actual modalities
- management financial reports (these do essentially the same as above)

C. Total Hours Required as per Classification
- accumulation of activities with predetermined time values
- tally of daily actual acuity required classification information

D. Total Hours of Care or Service Provided
- sum of the daily <u>actual</u> hours staffed
- payroll records: productive and nonproductive hours paid

The next several pages are devoted to forms that can be used to monitor and evaluate HPM targets: (1) Budgeted HPM, (2) Classified HPM, (3) Actual HPM.

Biweekly Classification Report

The purpose of the **Biweekly Classification Report**, Form 4.2-Example, is to log actual classified patient care or service hour requirements based on hours already approved for specific modalites. The top part of the form involves two steps:

(1) Daily: Log the number of complete and charged modalities, making sure that the total is equal to the number of days billed by the business office and the total modalities billed by the department that day.

(2) Biweekly: Calculate **total modalities** for each individual modality by adding the daily totals, and then multiply each total by the standard HPM for that modality, to identify the individual **total weighted/required hours** for the two-week period. Then total these columns to calculate biweekly **total modalities** and **total weighted/ required hours.**

Sections A and B of the bottom part of the form are completed by simply pulling down the sums of Total Modalities and Total Weighted/Required Hours from the top of the form. Also, the form is set up in a biweekly format to match a two-week payroll period so that data for part C are easily retrieved from already calculated, and most likely available, payroll information. Section D, **hours per modality,** tells the heart of the story. Reducing the data to hours per one modality magnifies the impact of the example's variances:

Comparing *actual (1.2)* **to** *classified (.8)*
How well were acuity needs met? A variance of .4 hours may not seem like a lot; but, in this case, it represents 24 minutes (on the average) of staff time expended beyond what was needed for every modality delivered during the period. The productivity index indicates 67% (target is 100%) showing actual staffing met and exceeded, by 33%, the classified acuity required HPM.

Comparing *actual (1.2)* **to** *budgeted (1.0)*
How well did we stay within budget and financial constraints? The productivity index indicates actual staffing 15% higher than what was budgeted per modality and it will impact direct costs by the same proportion. A budgeted labor cost per modality of $10 inflates to $11.50.

Comparing *classified (.8)* **to** *budgeted (1.0)*
Is the budget allocation adequate to meet actual patient care needs? At this point, yes, and with a little cushion. If the classified trend continues, standards should be examined to identify ways to improve the quality of services. As it stands, the staff could handle 20% more workload.

In Section E, productivity indexes are calculated. Looking at performance as a percent facilitates comparing departments to each other, regardless of size or HPM. The target performance is 100%.

Biweekly Classification Report

Modality Description and Charge Number	Sunday	Monday	Tuesday	Wednesday	Thursday	Friday	Saturday	Sunday	Monday	Tuesday	Wednesday	Thursday	Friday	Saturday	Total Modals	Hours per Modal (HPM)	Total Weighted/ Required Hours
OP Xray #1	20	10	10	10	20			20	10	10	15	15			140	.5	70
OP Xray #2	20		30	25	25				10	10	15	15			150	1.0	150
OP Xray #3			3		4			7	5		6	5			30	1.5	45
IP Xray #1	20	20	20	20	20			15	20	25	20	20			200	.5	100
IP Xray #2	5	5	5	5	10			5	5	5	5	10			60	1.0	60
IP Xray #3	4	8	6	4	5			10	6	4	7	6			60	1.5	90
TOTALS	69	43	74	64	84			57	56	54	68	71			640		515

A. Total pay period modalities **640**

B. Total weighted/required hours (from above) **515**

C. Total hours actually provided (Source: payroll, Productivity and   **740**
   Acuity Report, or a simple manual count of actual staffed hours)

D. Hours per modality (HPM):
   1) Budgeted (the standard remains constant throughout fiscal year)   **1.0**
   2) Weighted/required [B ÷ A]   **0.8**
   3) Actual provided (from above) [C ÷ A]   **1.2**

E. Productivity index (use figures from D1, D2, and D3 for formulas)

   1) Hours provided to hours budgeted: $\frac{\text{Hours Budgeted}}{\text{Hours Provided}}$ or $\frac{\text{D1}}{\text{D3}}$ **83%**

   2) Actual to weighted/required: $\frac{\text{Hours Weighted/Required}}{\text{Hours Provided}}$ or $\frac{\text{D2}}{\text{D3}}$ **67%**

Form 4.2-Example

Biweekly Classification Report

Modality Description and Charge Number	Sunday	Monday	Tuesday	Wednesday	Thursday	Friday	Saturday	Sunday	Monday	Tuesday	Wednesday	Thursday	Friday	Saturday	Total Modals	Hours per Modal (HPM)	Total Weighted/ Required Hours
TOTALS																	

A. Total pay period modalities _____

B. Total weighted/required hours (from above) _____

C. Total hours actually provided (Source: payroll, Productivity and Acuity Report, or a simple manual count of actual staffed hours) _____

D. Hours per modality (HPM):
   1) Budgeted (the standard remains constant throughout fiscal year) _____
   2) Weighted/required [B ÷ A] _____
   3) Actual provided (from above) [C ÷ A] _____

E. Productivity index (use figures from D1, D2, and D3 for formulas)

   1) Hours provided to hours budgeted: $\frac{\text{Hours Budgeted}}{\text{Hours Provided}}$ or $\frac{D1}{D3}$ _____

   2) Actual to weighted/required: $\frac{\text{Hours Weighted/Required}}{\text{Hours Provided}}$ or $\frac{D2}{D3}$ _____

Form 4.2

Productivity Worksheet & Analysis

There are two advantages of being able to analyze acuity, budget, and actual performance data concurrently. It enables you (1) to react quickly, making adjustments that impact quality and productivity outcomes; and (2) to prepare and update superiors *before* they get other financial reports. If, for example, in the outpatient department—a normally stable and high-revenue-producing department—a routine volume of modalities is experienced during a period but with a disproportionate amount of labor cost, it would probably catch the eye and concern of the administrator responsible for outpatient services. Some managers would prefer to know this information first so they are prepared to answer the inevitable question, "What's going on?" or even better, answer before it's asked by sending the information on **Productivity Worksheet & Analysis**, Form 4.3 (an abbreviated version of the **Biweekly Classification Report**, Form 4.2), to superiors at the end of the current period. The possible reasons are numerous; but,

assuming the manager performed competently, the answers to "What's going on?" might be (1) a larger proportion of high-acuity modalities than was projected in the budget was ordered; (2) new personnel, who are not yet up to target productivity levels, are providing services; (3) physicians have unrealistic expectations of what's to be done during outpatient procedures, or (4) equipment breakdown is causing increased waiting time, rework, and patient dissatisfaction.

These possibilities all involve the quality of service and the productivity of staff. And it's the manager, armed with documentation, who is in the best position to address these issues. Maybe the new equipment that was previously requested, and denied, will now

---

Productivity Worksheet & Analysis*

Department: <u>*Cath Lab*</u> Prepared by: <u>*J. Greenfield*</u>
Pay Period Beginning: <u>*Sunday, June 1*</u>

A. Total period modalities: <u>*132*</u>

B. Total hours required as per budget: <u>*528*</u>

C. Total hours required as per classification: <u>*660*</u>

D. Total hours of care or service provided: <u>*620*</u>
(Source: payroll department or sum of daily actual staffed hours)

E. Hours per modality (HPM):

　1. Budgeted
　　As approved for the fiscal year (B ÷ A): <u>*4.0*</u>

　2. Classified
　　Hours required per classification data ÷ actual modalities (C ÷ A): <u>*5.0*</u>

　3. Actual
　　Hours actually staffed and provided ÷ actual modalities (D ÷ A): <u>*4.7*</u>

F. Productivity indexes (use figures from E1, E2, and E3 for formulas):

　1. Hours provided to hours budgeted (E1 ÷ E3): <u>*85%*</u>
$$\frac{\text{Hours Budgeted}}{\text{Hours Provided}}$$

　2. Actual to weighted/required (E2 ÷ E3): <u>*106%*</u>
$$\frac{\text{Hours Weighted/Required}}{\text{Hours Provided}}$$

Form 4.3-Example　　　　* *Data Source: Productivity & Acuity Report, Form 4.1*

Productivity Worksheet & Analysis*

Department: _____ Prepared by: _____
Pay Period Beginning: _____

A. Total period modalities: _____

B. Total hours required as per budget: _____

C. Total hours required as per classification: _____

D. Total hours of care or service provided: _____
(Source: payroll department or sum of daily actual staffed hours)

E. Hours per modality (HPM):

1. **Budgeted**
   As approved for the fiscal year (B ÷ A): _____

2. **Classified**
   Hours required per classification data ÷ actual modalities (C ÷ A): _____

3. **Actual**
   Hours actually staffed and provided ÷ actual modalities (D ÷ A): _____

F. Productivity indexes (use figures from E1, E2, and E3 for formulas):

1. Hours provided to hours budgeted (E1 ÷ E3): _____

$$\frac{\text{Hours Budgeted}}{\text{Hours Provided}}$$

2. Actual to weighted/required (E2 ÷ E3): _____

$$\frac{\text{Hours Weighted/Required}}{\text{Hours Provided}}$$

have sufficient documentation of need. Physician expectations that seem unachievable can be negotiated, marketed, repriced, and budgeted. And, finally, if acuities and corresponding labor requirements aren't reflected in prices and revenue, it's time to look at restructuring your prices.

The productivity indexes are particularly interesting because managers can compare departments of different sizes without distortion. Even more important, the performance rating of a unit can be tracked, even though its volume of activity may change significantly from one period to the next. The budgeted/provided index tells how well actual hours match what was budgeted, and the weighted/ provided data tell how well actual hours match the classified needed hours. In both cases the optimal situation is 100 percent agreement.

All of the monitoring forms are easy to use and can be completed quickly. Some managers delegate this task to staff members to give them a better understanding of department productivity goals; others delegate to clerks, and as many others won't give it up at all because it provides them, in almost a moment, with a picture of the volume and intensity of activity in the department.

Quick Indicators of Productivity Success

There are two key indicators of a department's productivity performance that can say a lot at a glance. The now familiar hours per modality (HPM) is the keystone of the budget and, therefore, appears on most management reports. Managers can see quickly if the hours actually paid during the period are above or below target. The same is true with Salary Cost per Modality, but with the added advantage of seeing the dollar impact of their decisions. For example, if a manager has utilized a lot of overtime during a period, it may or may not show up when looking at the HPM targets, but it will definitely show up when total actual salary costs are split between actual modalities. Drawing on an example used earlier in the section, consider the department budgeted for 44,000 modalities at 1.0 HPM. If the average salary is $10.00 per hour (selected for ease of calculation, not professional significance) then the total salary budget, for direct care or services, would be $440,000 (44,000 modalities x 1.0 HPM x $10.00 average salary) or $10.00 per modality. The chart on the next page, **Budget: Based on Projected Modalities** shows how these two indicators break down into monthly projections.

Projected Modalities:	*44,000*
Approved Hours per Modality:	*1.0*
Average Salary:	*$10.00 per hour*
Total Budgeted Cost:	*$440,000*
Salary Cost (Direct) per Modality:	*$10.00*

Budget: Based on
Projected Modalities

(A)	(B)	(C)	(D)	(E)	(F)
Month	Projected Modalities	Budget HPM	Direct Hours Worked (column B x C)	Budgeted Salary Cost (column D x $10*)	Salary Cost per Modality (column E ÷ B)
JAN	4800	1.0	4800	$ 48,000	$ 10.00
FEB	4400	1.0	4400	$ 44,000	$ 10.00
MAR	4000	1.0	4000	$ 40,000	$ 10.00
APR	3600	1.0	3600	$ 36,000	$ 10.00
MAY	3200	1.0	3200	$ 32,000	$ 10.00
JUN	3200	1.0	3200	$ 32,000	$ 10.00
JUL	2800	1.0	2800	$ 28,000	$ 10.00
AUG	2800	1.0	2800	$ 28,000	$ 10.00
SEP	3600	1.0	3600	$ 36,000	$ 10.00
OCT	4400	1.0	4400	$ 44,000	$ 10.00
NOV	4000	1.0	4000	$ 40,000	$ 10.00
DEC	3200	1.0	3200	$ 32,000	$ 10.00
Totals	44,000	1.0	44,000	$440,000	$10.00

Assuming an average hourly salary of $10.00 per hour.

The chart above shows projected expectations and targets. The chart on the opposite page shows actual performance. Monthly accumulation of actual data provides quick indicators of productivity and financial performance to the department manager. Each month, after performing the simple mathematical calculations shown, the manager can see if the HPM and the Salary Costs per Modality have remained on target. The annual variance percentages have been calculated; and, as you can see, the percentages vary considerably. Note that these variances are based solely on volume, without regard for acuity. The department manager, using these quick indicators, should already have a feel for the acuity; and questionable variances should always be investigated further. See if you can identify the two months that are on target for both HPM and Salary Cost, based on the budget projections above. The answer is in the footnote on the next page.[15]

None of the forms or indicators that were reviewed in this section will produce information that is a surprise to the manager, because most managers know, sometimes only in their gut, what's going on. However, the tools will provide documentation, tracking capability, and measurable data managers can use to pursue quality and productivity goals with the staff members in their department.

Actual Performance: Based on Actual Modalities Accrued

(A)	(B)	(C)	(D)	(E)	(F)
Month	Actual Modalities Accrued	Actual Direct Hours Worked (from Payroll)	Direct HPM (C ÷ B)	Total Actual Salary Cost (from Payroll)	Salary Cost per Modality (E ÷ B)
JAN	3500	3000	.9	$ 30,000	$ 8.57
FEB	2000	3000	1.5	$ 30,000	$ 15.00
MAR	3000	3000	1.0	$ 30,000	$ 10.00
APR	2500	3000	1.2	$ 30,000	$ 12.00
MAY	2000	3000	1.5	$ 30,000	$ 15.00
JUN	2000	2000	1.0	$ 25,000	$ 12.50
JUL	2000	2000	1.0	$ 20,000	$ 10.00
AUG	1500	1000	.7	$ 10,000	$ 6.66
SEP	1500	1000	.7	$ 12,000	$ 8.00
OCT	2500	2000	.8	$ 20,000	$ 8.00
NOV	2500	3000	1.2	$ 30,000	$ 12.00
DEC	1500	2000	1.3	$ 20,000	$ 13.33
Totals	26,500	28,000	1.1	$287,000	$ 10.83
	40% Under Target		10% Over Target		8.3% Over Target

---

[15] The months of March and July hit both targets: 1.0 HPM at a salary cost of $10.00 per modality. June was on target for HPM, but had overtime utilization that drove the salary cost up to $12.50 per modality.

To lead the people walk behind them

Lao-Tsu

Section 5

Leadership: The Key to Quality & Productivity Results

The Chinese philosopher, Lao-Tse, had some powerful and insightful thoughts on leadership, which were put beautifully into verse by Witter Bynner.[16]

A leader is best
When people barely know he exists.
Not so good when people obey and acclaim him,
Worse, when they despise him.
"Fail to honor people, They fail to honor you";
But of a good leader, who talks little,
When his work is done, his aim fulfilled,
they will say, "we did it ourselves."

Leaders are developed, not born. Having the knack to seek out new opportunities, setting a standard of excellence, and inspiring a group of people to achieve a particular goal are not gifts from the gods. Strong leadership requires both technical and behavioral skills, including knowledge, risk, role modeling, caring, and *practice*. The best leaders seek out new opportunities for quality and productivity and inspire others with a desire to cooperate in the planning and implementation of the new opportunities. Even though it takes a tremendous amount of work and personal effort (like the frequent throwing of your ego in the trash masher), it is worth it! It is also comforting to know, on frustrating days, that the experiences, even the terrible ones, help build and mold leadership ability, skills, and a valuable personal reference library of experiences. Like all other achievements, it's a matter of persistence . . . and persistence always pays off.

---

[16] Aaron Levinson, J.D., "Art and Science of Supervision," Supervisor Nurse, June 1979, pp. 66-67. Note change in the spelling of Lao-Tse from previous page. Each time I looked at a new reference there was a different spelling. Rather than try to resolve the mystery, I used the spelling as cited in the particular reference.

Healthcare, like many other technically-based professions, has probably had few of its members enter their profession with leadership as their ultimate goal. Many excellent care providers have been promoted to managerial positions because of their clinical or technical skills, rather than their management skills (or interest), as it was once the only way to promotion and more money.[17] Some departments, nursing in particular, have implemented clinical promotion programs; but, for most healthcare workers, management is the only track to promotion. Competition for these management positions has increased considerably because of (1) a trend toward leaner management structures and broader spans of control, (2) graduates of hospital administration spilling over from the overcrowded administrative market into department-level positions, and (3) intensifying pressure and expectations of the individuals in these key management positions. Technically and clinically prepared candidates facing stiff competition, seasoned working managers overwhelmed with additional responsibilities, and managers working on continuous improvement are all asking, "How can I be a better leader and manager?"

Managing the efficient delivery of care at the desired level of quality is central to answering that question, and the skillful use of a combination of management and leadership skills can be instrumental in making it happen. Managers must become effective leaders, seeking out new opportunities for improving quality and productivity and inspiring others to support and actively participate in the planning, organizing, implementation, and evaluation of selected strategies.

Proactive & Reactive Leaders

The environment in healthcare today has brought out two, somewhat polarized, styles of leadership. *Reactive leaders* cite the problems of inflation, high energy costs, government intervention, etc. and place the blame for less than target quality and productivity on those factors that are, obviously, outside their realm of control. To some extent, that blame is correctly placed. Yes, there are external variables that we as healthcare managers cannot control; yet, it is also an excuse for the reactive leader who lacks the insight to anticipate developments and trends and who chooses to react or cope with problems, rather than meet them head on.

Proactive leaders, on the other hand, don't hide behind the uncontrollable external variables. Instead they use them to stimulate creativity, identifying what needs to be done and getting on with it. Proactive leaders have a positive way of

---

[17] This is similar to any technical or specialty area and does not usually create a problem. Usually if an individual is great at providing patient care, he or she is probably achievement-oriented and can, therefore, be great at anything, if given the right leadership, training, and direction.

looking at the organization. It's not that they gloss over or are unaware of negative aspects; they'd just rather look for windows of opportunity than pout, whine, and complain. They anticipate more, risk more, and believe in choosing, rather than reacting to, an alternative; and they foster this style in their own staff. In the healthcare environment where processes are designed, implemented, and operated by people, both quality and productivity are bound to be significantly and directly impacted by employees managing and operating these systems. Proactive leaders capitalize on this situation by maintaining a positive, supportive, participative relationship with their employees. And it works!

Key Result Areas (KRAs)[18]

Vilfredo Pareto, an Italian economist who lived and studied in the 1800s, discovered a theory of distribution that remains popular and relevant today. The Pareto principle states "that the critical elements in any set usually constitute the minority of the elements. This is also called the 80-20 rule. 80 percent of the value is accounted for by 20 percent of the items."[19]   As an economist, he discovered that 80 percent of the wealth in his community was held by only 20 percent of the

> ## *THE PARETO PRINCIPLE*
>
> *20 percent of our time and effort*
> *produces 80 percent*
> *of the results*
>
> *- Vilfredo Pareto*

---

[18] I first heard this phrase at the seminar, "Inventory on Productivity and Performance Improvement (IPPI)," given by V. Clayton Sherman, Ed.D., in 1981. He has developed, with the help of Ann R. Sherman, M.S., a wonderful self-audit instrument for managers that includes tests, answers, discussion booklets, and an administration manual. I personally, found the tool enlightening and informative and recommend it highly. More information can be obtained from Beta Group, Ltd., 24 North Emerson Street, Mt. Prospect, Ill. 60056, (312) 398-1277.

[19] Merrill E. Douglass, *The Time Management Workbook*. Time Management Center, 7612 Florissant Road, St. Louis, Mo. 63121.

people. In your healthcare organization, you might discover that 80 percent of your revenue comes from 20 percent of your patients, 80 percent of your profit comes from 20 percent of the modalities you offer, 80 percent of your problems comes from 20 percent of your patients (or staff), and 80 percent of your effectiveness comes from 20 percent of the things that you do. The question is: Do you know what the things are that constitute your 20 percent?

> ## *What are your key responsibilities and are they receiving 80% of your time and effort?*
>
> - *Quality and patient satisfaction*
> - *Productivity and expense control*
> - *Innovation*
> - *Staff development*
> - *Organizational development*

Theories that stay around and receive such frequent mention as the *Pareto Principle* do so because they are so often right. Proactive managers—those who consistently meet their objectives head on and achieve them—identify the most important 20 percent of their responsibilities and then stay tenaciously focused on them until goals are achieved. There are, however, many external and internal variables that pull the manager's attention from his or her key responsibilities. Internally, there are magnets—such as conflict, crises, and incongruent priorities of patients, staff, administration, and the medical staff. Externally, third party payers, business and industry, and government agencies have their priorities too. The list can be endless; and it becomes a challenge, in itself, for the healthcare manager to stay focused and attentive to the key responsibilities of his or her department. It is easy to get sidetracked, to look up from our work and discover that we have become totally absorbed in a time-consuming, but insignificant, activity.

Which one(s) of your key responsibilities relates to quality and productivity management? They all do. All key responsibilities deserving of our focus relate, directly or indirectly, to optimizing quality within cost and productivity constraints. But managers, no matter how great, can't do this alone. The key to quality and productivity results lies in our leadership and how we involve our staff members in this effort. The remainder of this section will be devoted to the specifics of getting staff actively involved with the puruit of quality and productivity results and how managers can make the most of their contribution.

Communication & Participation

Volumes have been written on the benefits of Japanese management, participative management style, and good communication methods. The reason is simple ...they produce results. For the most part, our employees are just like us; that is, they want to do a good job and they care about their performance. Our organizations and systems should be set up for *these* individuals, not the exceptions. Consider the table below, which shows the results of a survey that has been given to thousands of workers (some of the workers were also managers reporting to a higher level of management). Note that the three most important things to employees were perceived, by management, to be the least important to employees.[20]

WHAT WORKERS SAY THEY WANT		WHAT MANAGERS THINK WORKERS WANT
1	Full Appreciation of Work	8
2	Feeling of Being in on Things	10
3	Help with Personal Problems	9
4	Job Security	2
5	Good Pay	1
6	Interesting Work	5
7	Promotion and Growth	3
8	Loyalty to Employees	6
9	Good Work Conditions	4
10	Tactful Discipline	7

---

[20] From another great reference book: John W. Newstrom and Edward E. Scannell, *Games Trainers Play: Experiential Learning Exercises* (New York: McGraw-Hill Book Company, 1980). It has frequently saved me from being a boring teacher, something I consider a fate worse than death.

Employees can be instrumental in the success of a department's quality and productivity results, but involving them means more than just telling them what's going on and what they should do. Real communication, where there is talking and listening, will bring out the best ideas and results. Managers can improve communication techniques and increase involvement with some of these methods.

> *There's more to communication than talking*
>
> - *Create time to listen, giving undivided attention.*
> - *Concentrate; actively work at two-way communication*
> - *Delay evaluation, judging content not delivery.*
> - *Pay attention to nonverbal communication (body language, tone of voice, and facial expressions). It speaks louder than words.*
> - *Communicate strategies, views, ideas, and expectations (especially when times are tough) - and integrate employees' frustrations, fears, opinions, and ideas into decision making.*

In every business sector, including healthcare, there is renewed interest and recognition in the importance of the individual's talents, contributions, and potential. Considering the labor intensity and professionalism in healthcare organizations, the talents of the staff can be a powerful force. Rosabeth Kanter, author of *The Change Masters*, refers to staff as "the corporate entrepreneurs" and has produced more than sufficient evidence to substantiate that claim. After studying organizations in depth, she discovered that those with reputations for being progressive in their participative management style were also noticeably ahead of their competitors in long-term profitability and financial growth.[21]

> **Why get staff members involved? Because...**
> ...they have the expertise and necessary relevant information.
> ...they can add clarity to all aspects of the situation or topic.
> ...their participation will lead to better results and employee commitment.
>
> **When should staff members be involved? When...**
> ...the decision will influence quality.
> ...more information is needed.
> ...staff acceptance is important to results or could cause conflict.
> ...staff members are aware and supportive of organizational goals.

---

[21] Rosabeth Kanter, *The Change Masters* (New York: Simon and Schuster, 1983), pp. 17-23.

Creativity & Innovation

Creativity was once the private domain of those who were able to express themselves artistically. Lately, however, modern-day philosophers, and business executives too, have been reevaluating this assumption. Words, such as entrepreneurship, innovation, think tanks, and brainstorming, are popping up in business journals, board rooms, and even individual healthcare departments. Everyone is trying to come up with better ideas, and more efficient or effective methods, and asking questions such as "What's wrong?" "How can we fix it?" "How can we do it better?" and "How can we do it faster?" Today's problems cannot be solved with yesterday's solutions. And, as managers, we can either reminisce about the good old days or build on our experiences, challenge our own creativity, and find new answers, solutions, and ideas we might never have believed were possible.

What is creative thinking? Roger von Oech, creativity consultant and author, says that it's not the knowledge, but rather what you do with your knowledge, your attitude, and outlook, that makes you a creative thinker:

By changing perspective and playing
with our knowledge and experience,
we can make the ordinary extraordinary
and the unusual commonplace . . .
DISCOVERY
consists of looking at the same thing as everyone else
and thinking something different.[22]

— Roger von Oech

It pays off to take the risk. Your employees, as inhouse consultants, can play a significant role in this regard and no doubt are chomping at the bit, waiting for a brave manager to let them know the "unboundaries." You've probably heard them talking in the cafeteria saying things like, "Why doesn't management do this or that...?" When staff members are involved in setting and achieving goals, and ideas are shared, brainstormed, and developed with their participation, there is great potential for both quality and productivity improvements. Employees have

---

[22] Roger von Oech, *A Whack on the Side of the Head* (New York: Warner Books, 1983), p. 7.

the foresight into what will work and the enthusiasm to carry ideas to fruition. It's a natural fit, but they might be waiting for permission.

> ### *It's easier to get forgiveness than permission.*
>
> – author unknown

Managers can give this permission in a nonthreatening manner (and even have some fun) by doing the following:

(1) Conduct staff meetings devoted to solving quality problems and continuous improvement.

(2) Use brainstorming, a popular, easy technique used to inspire and gather creative ideas. It requires that every idea be heard, recorded, and seriously considered.

(3) Structure your department to support a creative approach. Let people know it's okay to report problems and mistakes because everyone can learn from them, and use team planning to correct or avoid the problem in the future.

You should think about and treat your staff members as a team, with you as the coach; it will spread the burden of departmental responsibility as well as the potential for achievement and recognition. When a manager opens the creativity doors—letting it be known that unusual, untraditional, even *bizarre* ideas will be considered—employees will begin to feel more comfortable stretching their own minds for different solutions.

Delegation

Asking staff members to participate in and, in effect, to take on, some of management's responsibilities, must be accompanied by a willingness to relinquish some of the authority. This can be very frightening, or it can be terrific if the manager fosters an environment where change and risk can happen. It's a lot like the routine mother birds go through when they nudge their babies out of the nest. Sometimes the babies falter, but eventually they do fly. Similarly, our staff members occasionally need a nudge too. And they don't always get winning results the first time they're delegated additional responsibilities. But with practice and a supportive framework they will develop, and results will continue to grow. Managers play a key role in setting the stage for success or failure. Here are some ideas that can help the delegation process work with positive results.

When you delegate...

- *Make sure goals are mutually agreed on before you begin.*

- *Tell participating employees why the job is important, why it needs to be done, and why they were chosen to do it.*

- *Delegate in terms of results...but let the employees decide **how** to get them.*

- *Give (define) authority and constraints at the start.*

- *Plan controls; ask for specific feedback and preschedule routine progress reviews.*

Motivation

We've assumed, throughout this section, that employees want to get involved in improving quality and productivity, but that may not always be the case. Sometimes employees may feel management is dumping on them or that they have enough to do without doing management's job too. Managers are responsible for motivating their employees to accomplish quality and productivity goals. Allowing them to participate in decision making and problem solving will motivate some employees; but, as motivational theorist Frederick Herzberg has pointed out, different things motivate different people. Managers who have taken the time to discover what motivates each of their staff members are in the best position to mobilize them to action, and satisfaction in their work. Herzberg calls this action "vertical job loading" and feels it is an ideal way to make jobs more fulfilling for the employee. He has written many timeless articles on motivation and designed the chart, on the following page, as a demonstration of the vertical job loading theory in a 1968 article for the <u>Harvard Business Review</u>.[23]

---

[23] Frederick Herzberg, "One More Time: How Do You Motivate Employees?" <u>Harvard Business Review</u> 46, no. 1 (1968): 59.

Principles of Job Enrichment
by Vertical Job Loading

Motivations	Principle
Responsibility, Achievement	Remove controls while retaining accountability
Responsibility and Recognition	Increase individual's accountability for own work
Responsibility, Achievement and Recognition	Assign a complete unit of work, start to finish, or Grant more authority/freedom within work activity
Internal Recognition	Make pertinent management reports available for review
Growth and Learning	Introduce new and more difficult tasks
Responsibility, Growth, and Advancement	Assign individuals specific or specialized tasks, enable them to become the department "experts"

It is management's responsibility to find
preexisting winning qualities in staff members,
to bring those qualities to the individual's attention, and then
to work with the staff member to build on that base.
Once people discover they can choose to be a winner, and
in fact have their own cheerleader and mentor,
they become insatiable for achievement.

The task for management is to find out what motivates people and then focus on assigning responsibilities and tasks accordingly. What is drudgery to one person may be exciting and interesting to another. The obstacle is that managers may not know what motivates their staff; and, in fact, just as often employees don't know themselves. Motivations change at different periods of life depending on values and life experiences. For example, an individual highly motivated by achievement and the work itself may suddenly be motivated by money alone after becoming a single parent solely responsible for the support of two children. Herzberg cites 16 different items that can either be job satisfiers or job dissatisfiers. **Satisfiers** will always motivate people, but **dissatisfiers** (a.k.a. hygiene or maintenance factors) will only motivate people if they are absent. For example, an employee who knows there is a line of others waiting for his or her job is more likely to be motivated by the promise of job security than an employee who knows they can't be replaced.

It's vitally important for management to know what motivates employees ...and to also know what motivates themselves, as managers. All of Herzberg's factors have been arranged in a grid on the following page to provide an exercise and motivational assessment tool for both management and staff. It looks like a puzzle, but it's no game. It is a revealing self-evaluation tool that can help individuals discover what it is that motivates them and then make decisions about their life, in light of the new information.

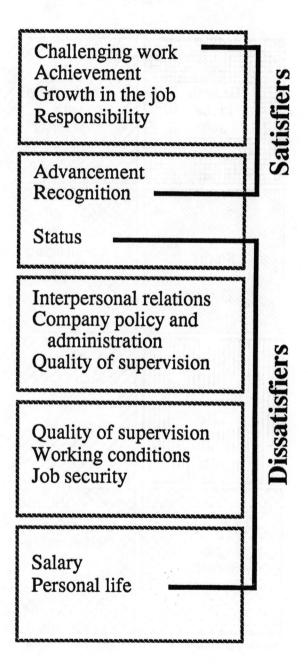

Herzberg's Two-Factor Theory

Challenging work
Achievement
Growth in the job
Responsibility

Advancement
Recognition

Status

Interpersonal relations
Company policy and
  administration
Quality of supervision

Quality of supervision
Working conditions
Job security

Salary
Personal life

Satisfiers

Dissatisfiers

Hints for the "What Motivates You?" Exercise

Here are a few hints to help you make the most of this exercise. First, lock yourself in a quiet space; decisions may be made that significantly affect your future. Second, divide the pieces into groups of four: highest priority, lowest priority and two in between. It is easier to fine tune between the categories, but don't be

What Motivates You?

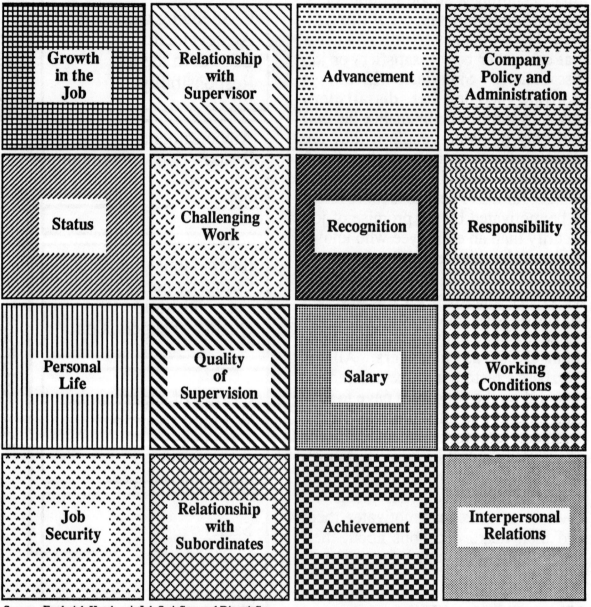

Source: Frederick Herzberg's Job Satisfiers and Dissatisfiers.

Directions: *1. Copy; cut into single squares*
2. Think, ponder, reflect, etc.
3. Rank in order of priority

surprised if you move back and forth among groups before finalizing your list. Third, if every item or even two items seem indistinguishable, ask yourself how would you feel if you didn't have it? Example: "Money is not all that important to me… but, how would I feel about this job if I wasn't being paid?"

Management & Staff Development

Last, but not least, managers need to take a leadership role in developing their staff and themselves. Naturally, finding bright, talented people and placing them in the correct position both play an important role in this process; but management and staff development activities that follow the hiring process can make the most significant difference.

The long-range goal of preparing and grooming both staff and management personnel is twofold; that is, to improve (1) the quality of the service and (2) the efficiency of the method of delivery. Participative management is a proven and successful method of achieving this goal because everyone has a share in the decision-making process and senses a feeling of shared responsibility for the outcomes. Employees evolve, as a result of this responsibility, into individuals who "think like managers," which creates a powerfully positive force and gives managers an even stronger base on which to build a participative management arrangement in their department.

However, before shifting such a large responsibility to staff members, management must prepare them to meet the challenge. Managers who are secure that their staff can make correct and appropriate decisions are going to be much more comfortable and likely to delegate and have staff participate in decision making. Thus, the more information and techniques that management shares with staff, the more equipped the staff will be to make good decisions. On the next page there are some ideas to help managers enhance and participate in the growth and development of their staff.

How to Bring Out
the Best in Your Staff

Hire the right people for the job.

Share responsibility for growth, education, and development.

> • *Be a mentor; groom and prepare staff and invest in them.*
> • *Beware they'll appreciate while the equipment depreciates.*
> • *Have "winner" role models do the training/development.*

Negotiate expectations and responsibilities.

> • *Note where discipline will come into play.*
> • *Spell out rewards and how to earn them.*
>> - *Pay for performance with management incentives.*
>> - *Promote for performance (clinical and management).*
>> - *Have clear, fair, competency-based job opportunities.*
>> - *Give frequent recognition.*

Involve employees in setting and deciding how to achieve goals.

> • *Don't just talk about participative management . . . do it!*
>> - *Use team building and group work to solve problems.*
>> - *Give "scoop" first hand...so staff feels in on things.*
>> - *Stay in touch, wander, and talk to corporate entrepreneurs who can fix a problem before it becomes one.*

> • *Show staff members their opinions matter. Act on their suggestions:*
>> - *quality circles*   - *meetings with management*
>> - *hot lines*   - *suggestion committees*

If you believe your employees can do anything...they can! Give them the opportunity to experience the same feeling of achievement that ignites your enthusiasm.

Section 6

Ideas for Improving
Quality & Productivity

It only takes one spark to get a fire going; ideas are just as contagious and explosive. Even those ideas that are only average when they're first discussed seem to grow as more and more people look at them from different angles and add their input. And sometimes they become *terrific*. At other times, ideas spark other ideas that are completely different, but are great nonetheless as a solution to the problem or situation at hand or maybe some other problem. Looking at ideas and discussing them with a group of people will stimulate creative thinking and a brainstorming approach to managing that will generate even more ideas and alternatives. The more alternatives available, the more opportunity managers and employees have to pick the one that will best meet their needs. Brainstorming activities should be ongoing, and that is what this section is all about... ideas...lots of different kinds of ideas to read and review when creativity is at a low ebb or even just to see if someone else has already done the legwork and thought of a new idea for you.[24]

Case Study: A cardiac rehabilitation department successfully survived a budget reduction because a variety of creative ideas were implemented, including: (1) streamlined standards of care and performance, (2) supportive written materials, (3) videotapes, and (4) focused patient care outcomes. Shortly thereafter, another budget reduction was mandated; and the staff members were frustrated because they had already used all of their great ideas. The manager decided to get the group together anyway, primarily to let them air their fears and frustrations. But to everyone's surprise a brilliant idea emerged from the group's discussions when one of the staff members came up with the idea of using a checklist for charting.

---

[24] Sources for the ideas in this section are voluminous and beyond my memory as I have gathered them from years of reading, research, and teaching (in both university and hospital settings). I do, however, remember that I picked up many of the work simplification ideas from the **Miami VA Medical Center** in Miami, Florida. I would like to thank the nurse managers who, in spite of their skepticism, tapped their staff for work simplification and streamlining ideas. The cumulative list added up to over 100 ideas for doing things better and faster.

They decided that they could list everything they would ever want to tell physicians about a patient's progress on one piece of paper (leaving a space to write anything extraordinary), print it, and use it for routine charting. It took them 2 minutes to fill out the checklist, instead of the 15 minutes it took to write everything down; and the quality improved because they were giving physicians far more information than was provided with the old method. Quality and Productivity can be done!

Work Simplification & Streamlining

If your budgeted patient care or service HPM are approved for less than you requested or if there is a budget cut of FTEs without a corresponding reduction in volume, it will mean, ultimately, that the staff will have less time to accomplish its workload. Although there may be ample documentation to justify the additional care or service hours, in some organizations the funding cannot be approved financially. Healthcare managers can continue to complain and try to justify the need, but that won't help the staff deal with the situation or ensure the service is delivered at an acceptable level. A proactive and positive way of handling such a situation is to brainstorm with staff members on ways to save time without compromising the predetermined quality standards. Let them know you are aware of their workload dilemma, but help them work through it to deliver the highest level of quality within the cost constraints. It may mean *changing* your standards, but that doesn't have to be the equivalent of *lowering* them.

√ Review each activity and procedure with the staff to analyze if it can be done better/faster.

√ Tape some or all change-of-shift reports. Use a standardized, systematic report format.

√ Check out different ways of charting notes, using a checklist format or computer support.

√ Prioritize. Identify the most important aspects of each patient's care. Do those things first.

√ Consolidate and help each other. Teamwork works!

√ Communicate. Make good use of management and staff meetings, logs, and bulletin boards. Talk about quality and productivity issues and seek solutions.

√ Have employees who do things *better and faster* develop policies and procedures and orient new employees.

√ Examine the advantages and disadvantages of computerization:
  • Documentation of patient care or related services
  • Data collection for quality assurance, budget, performance management

- Computers that requisition medications and supply items
- Staff development, inservice, and skill building

√ Reallocate inappropriate responsibilities to the departments that should be responsible. If, however, you've been receiving budget dollars for delivering those services, you might have to give those back too.

√ Use retirees and high school and university students as volunteers. Review job descriptions and check with volunteer coordinator for transferable duties:
  - Escorting patients
  - Working in the clinic
  - Taking temperatures
  - Passing out water
  - Running errands
  - Making beds

√ Ensure that staff has a working knowledge of policies and procedures and that policies and procedures are designed to be efficient as well as effective.

√ Make use of a management engineer who can make recommendations regarding:
  - development of accurate work standards (unit of service: HPM).
  - use of HPM for budget goals, productivity targets, and classification systems.
  - analysis, adjustment, and improvement of methods, work distribution, and work flow.

√ Use operations analysis to ensure the effectiveness of operations and take appropriate corrective action when indicated. Specific activities involved in operations analysis include:
  - Evaluating performance in light of goals set by management
  - Pinpointing weakness in operations and improving organizational effectiveness
  - Selecting cost-containment priorities and opportunities
  - Identifying differences between policy and practice
  - Identifying inappropriate policy
  - Analyzing financial data
  - Interviewing management

√ Schedule patients and activities using a systematic method that works.

√ Avoid duplicate efforts. Are two departments doing the same thing? Collaborate to save time.

√ Integrate family members into patient care. Explain the importance of their role (responsibility), now and after discharge.

√ Use task forces (also known as *self-destruct committees*) to get specific tasks accomplished. They are notorious for getting the job done and disbanding. If the group has worked well together and enjoys the responsibility, give them the option of moving on to a new project.

√ Look at organizational structure. Do policies support a cost-contained but quality-based productivity system?

√ Always delegate to the lowest level to save time and money.

√ Dictate patient care notes - from a pocket dictating machine.

√ Budget for telephones or pocket page units that could be easily carried by employees.

√ Other ideas: _____

_____

_____

_____

_____

Strategic Planning & Marketing

Marketing has become a serious consideration in every healthcare institution as the competition for the healthcare dollar continues to intensify. Marketing professionals tell providers that times have changed and that we can no longer decide what is best for patients and then force it on them. Rather, we must discover what the purchaser of healthcare (including patient, physician, or third party payer) wants and then develop our strategic plans to provide it to the market. Strategic planning is organizational planning based on uncontrollable external variables, which include the existing market basket data. Managers in healthcare organizations are in various stages of realizing that their orgranizations are part of a healthcare system, rather than the system itself, and many factors within the system affect their plans for the future.

Strategic Planning

√ Use the expert knowledge of your staff members for strategic planning purposes. They can:
  • develop departmental objectives compatible with long-range organizational goals.
  • assess the external market situation.
  • analyze internal considerations (e.g., cost and resource impacts).
  • develop specific project objectives, implementation strategies, and target dates.

√ Make organizational goals the goals of every employee by:
  • planning with them and identifying ways they, as individuals, can contribute to achieving departmental and organizational goals.
  • including their personal contribution as part of the performance appraisal system.

Marketing

√ Participate in community activities, spectator events, and community service. Decentralize and organize resources out to the community at a cost it can afford. Recognize that hospitals with strong community ties will do better businesswise. Do the same internally. To the extent possible, have a department representative on hospital committees and involved in significant activities.

√ Stay with what you know and do best, where you have the edge, and take small but educated risks to enhance the chance of success. Then develop your strategy and market! market! market! Use your own employees when possible; they make great marketing professionals.

√ Read public relations newsletters. Hospital PR staff members always brag about their institution and you might pick up a really great idea.

√ Be aware that the market will be shrinking as the patient's economic responsibility increases.

√ Develop brochures; they tell your whole story, create a desired image, and can be used for patient information or education. Use them whenever possible.

√ Know who your clients are (e.g., patients, physicians, third party payers, HMOs and PPOs, businesses, other departments within the organization) and their order of priority.

√ Beware of patient perspective. A patient survey regarding the patient's choice of hospitals showed:
   • 45% felt that they—the patient—had control over the choice of hospitals.
   • 28% felt that patient and physician decide together or negotiate.
   • 27% felt that it was physician choice alone (was 65% in 1978).

√ Be aware that patients expect technology and clinical competence as routine; so, their evaluation of care is often based on the hotel/human aspects. If you don't believe it, adopt one of your patients and see for yourself. Then work toward having terrific guest relations. It appears to take more care hours (i.e., money), but it's worth it and some say it saves money in the long run.

√ Use the bill to demonstrate if you're providing more nursing care than competitive hospitals.

√ Focus on wellness, health promotion, and fitness programs. And practice what you preach. It's a trend that is here to stay, and we'll do better in the wellness business than in the sickness business. Increased competition has brought wellness programs, patient education, and home care to center stage as "new and innovative" ideas, but many healthcare practitioners have been pushing for these programs for years.

√ Other ideas: _____

_____

_____

_____

_____

Program Planning

Program planning can guide the work of the institution and provide the direction for major planning decisions. For example, management in a healthcare organization with a major trauma center may be more willing to approve the start up of a STAT Laboratory than management in another institution that does not provide this service. Because financial success may depend on the volume of services (usually as volume increases, the potential to maximize profit and optimize quality increases), it is becoming increasingly more important to look at the feasibility of capturing a market, such as—cardiology, oncology, or obstetrics—as services are being analyzed for start up or continuation. Strategic thinkers are looking at major product lines, rather than individual service, resulting in an increase in the importance of program planning. Healthcare managers have been doing the program planning in healthcare institutions all along, so this is not new or threatening. As managers add marketing and financial skills to their repertoire, they have a terrific opportunity to become strategic planners for their own programs.

√ Pursue home care projects. They are proven winners and will only increase in utilization.

√ Collaborate with department stores on wellness and patient education counters or boutiques.

√ Develop community education opportunities:
  - risk factor screening and education
  - traveling health assessment van for screening and community education
  - blood pressure testing

√ Conduct on-site general screenings and assessments:
  - When needed, patients will be referred to:
    - personal physician
    - physician referral service (in the event of no personal physician)
  - Physician has the benefit of a complete report when patients come for their checkup.

√ Diversify within your area of expertise. Evaluate opportunities for outpatient day care in all of your already successful programs to ascertain their marketability to your community and potential to generate new programs and business.
  - geriatric
  - diabetic
  - psychiatric
  - pain treatment
  - child day care and sick child day care

√ Begin discharge planning and coordination the day the patient is admitted.
  - Even better, preadmission testing can identify potential problems before admission.
  - Reward nurses for their contribution to speeding up patient discharges.

√ Encourage and support joint hospital/physician ventures which make physicians the "gate-keepers" for control of resources as they share in the profits and losses.

√ Develop an economic grand rounds program (concept created by the American Medical Association): It will enhance physician awareness of the costs by looking at both the clinical and fiscal issues associated with a particular case history. Here are some changes that took place as a result of economic grand rounds:
  • Physicians ordered STAT laboratory work less because specimen pickup, delivery, and reporting times were changed to more convenient hours.
  • Preadmission testing was used more often.
  • Tests run for official, but erroneous, reasons (such as JCAHO required it) were stopped.
  • "Paneling of tests" was used automatically, whenever it saved on costs.

√ Compete enthusiastically with outside ventures. Competitors for ambulatory surgery, outpatient care, women's care, home care followup, etc. may have been first; but additional competition can enrich everyone.

√ Consider, when you pick/plan new programs, not only the **system cost** but also how the programs will make use of current (perhaps overage of) resources.

√ Other ideas: _____

_____

_____

_____

_____

Resource Planning & Evaluation

Department managers budget for expenses according to target quality levels and projected volume of (1) patient care or (2) related service modalities. Expenses per modality are used to either help decide on the pricing structure, or to react to the predetermined cap set by the reimbursment agency. When expenses rise above the budgeted level, the result is reduced profit, reduced operating margin (for the not-for-profit institutions), or worse, unreimbursed cost...the dreaded red ink. Plans for monitoring and controlling resource costs should be initiated at the time of budget and followed up on every day, every shift of the fiscal year. Because salary costs are by far the largest healthcare expenditure and also the costs that are most often out of control, most of the following ideas address healthcare labor resources.

Staffing Policies

√ Use part-time staff:
- Consider 2-hour, 4-hour, 6-hour part-time support positions.
- Use *parts* of part-time and other weird arrangements that fit your department routine.
- Split a full-time position into three temporary (4-month), full-time positions - each use requires the same amount of hours

√ Examine shifts of varying lengths for full-time staff: 12-hour, 10-hour, 6-hour, 4-hour.

√ Spread vacations so that only two or three staff members are away at any one time to reduce overtime and maintain even coverage.

√ Create float pools of part-time and per diem workers.

√ Cross-train staff to other departments. (In one hospital, during the slow summer months, employees were given the choice of either downsizing or painting the hospital. It turned a potential morale buster into a morale and team spirit builder.)

√ Hire staff with "warranties" to ensure that they can do the job when hired as new graduates.

√ Boost morale and productivity by being open to investigating the feasibility of innovative/ flexible scheduling plans.

√ Consider flexible full-time hours (e.g., 32-hour work weeks).

√ Budget to facilitate and reward productivity:
- Place professional staff on salary rather than hourly pay option.
- Generate financial incentives for heavier workload (acuity or volume).
- Compensate by caseload and/or acuity.
- Contract for annual hours use as needed instead of scheduling weekly.

Budget Planning

√ Know your product. Maybe the desired level of quality isn't all that expensive after all.
- Identify and validate required HPM.
- Begin cost accounting. It helps identify financially feasible and/or attractive services.
- Find costs - know what your costs are and what they'd be at varying levels of quality.

√ Identify costs first, then direct efforts toward:
- decreasing cost while maintaining or improving quality.
- increasing efficiency while maintaining or improving quality.
- reducing required HPM while maintaining or improving quality.

√ Get the HPM you need. If you can't, use work simplification ideas to whittle the workload.

√ Use the standard HPM to budget, monitor, and evaluate within a flexible budgeting plan.

√ Establish fair and credible time standards and monitoring techniques for measuring quality-based productivity:
- Logging or work sampling can be used to identify time standards. Or, as an alternative predetermined industry-accepted standards can be used.
- Monitoring should be easy, timely, credible, and simple enough to implement at the departmental level.

Budget Monitoring & Control

√ Adjust staffing to the workload. If you can't, manipulate the workload (census) to staff availability.

√ Develop an annual productivity plan for each department that includes:
- expected volume of output, by procedure, to be produced by the department
- manpower per unit of output
- labor and nonlabor expense per unit of output
- amounts of overtime and sick time to be used
- an authorized staffing complement based on projected volume

√ Keep an ongoing profile of absenteeism and communicate results to staff.

√ Plan and organize for the most effective utilization of skilled labor.

√ Keep a handle on staff training and development:
- Set cost targets for orientation expenses. Monitor and correct them if necessary.
- Reduce salaries of new employees who don't meet stated skill level.
- Have new employees, who need extraordinary orientation because they can't meet agreed on performance standards, continue at reduced pay or at their own expense.
- Work out a reward formula to help pay expenses for classes and continuing education.

√ Find out why overtime is occurring and correct excesses. Make sure overtime is not due to management scheduling decisions.
- Could it be prevented through better organization?
- Is the individual productivity of the employee the problem?
- Is permission required? With predetermined acceptable reasons for approval?
- Is a specific tangible reason required and documented?
- Have salaried "no-punch-in" positions been considered?

√ Maintain and build flexibility into staffing to help meet budget and classification targets.

√ Determine staff reduction plans:
- Agree on great call-off plans.
- Ask employees about their preferences for being called off, cross-trained, floated, etc.
- Determine on-call pay policy - with call pay for whole 8 hours, or without pay for first 2 hours of the shift.
- Approve "hospital appreciated" leave of absence without loss of benefits.
- Make sure policies support what's being done with staff reductions.

    • Work with staff to develop a contingency plan for low volume; and, if downsizing is a possibility, plan for it in advance so employees know what will happen and can plan their own personal contingencies.

Supplies & Equipment

√ Take advantage of innovations in technology.

√ Use a supply cart for setting up patient care rooms, in advance.

√ Insist on a strong preventive maintenance program. Having equipment that works well will save time.

√ Include "amount of staff time saved" as a criterion for any new equipment purchases and select equipment that will unburden direct care/service hours and save time for the staff.

√ Have supplies and linen available and accessible to save steps and time.

√ Maintain adequate inventory levels for department supplies with sufficient order periods, which will assist staff efficiency rather than interrupt and create more work.

√ Consider seriously *any* labor-saving device or equipment.

√ Support and encourage a strong capital investment strategy.

√ Consider (always), or reconsider, the cost benefit of reusables versus disposables. This decision is usually made in central supply; however, managers of patient care departments can supply valuable information on the "benefit" side of this equation on behalf of their staff and the patient.

√ Other ideas: _____

_____

_____

_____

_____

Leadership & Communication

Great ideas are valuable only when they are brought into the organization and shared with all individuals involved in, and responsible for, achieving the organization's goals. Leadership continually seeks out opportunities for maintaining or enhancing quality and for increasing productivity. Communication provides the vehicle for leaders to inspire cooperation in the planning and implementation of those opportunities and to generate results. As you read the list, remember that you, the manager, are the leader as well and, therefore, are responsible for setting the tone and creating the vision.

√ Know your key responsibilities. Check often to see if you're focusing on results or activities.

√ Remember to think differently. Be creative, innovative, and flexible! Sometimes it's productive to even be bizarre, and it's fun.

√ Find a quiet place for paper work and planning. Practice and teach time management skills.

√ Read and write newsletters. They are time economizers and enable direct communication to and from large groups!

√ Send for booklets filled with innovative ideas, such as the **Innovator's Catalog.** [25]

√ Attend conferences - one new idea can pay for your trip and maybe a few more.

√ Read everything! Listen to tapes in the car. Form a reading group with colleagues so you can share clippings and "highlighted" articles.

√ Learn to dictate written communications.

√ Network for information. Talk to everyone and learn from their experiences. Always ask questions. It's the fastest, best way to get the information you want.

√ Ask constantly, "What's wrong?" "How can we fix it?" and "Can we fix it before it breaks?"

√ Call long-distance to someone who wrote an article or has a similar program. He or she will be glad to talk with you…it's probably why the article was written.

√ Inform and educate staff members about what you are doing and how you plan to get there, while there's still time for them to provide meaningful input.

√ Communicate plans to staff members; then use them as resources through teams, task forces, and quality circles.

√ Look around - staff members are your best consultants; so, consult your "experts."
   • Ideas are more valuable than money.
   • People support what they help create.
   • All humans can think - management doesn't necessarily or always do it best.
   • If you want productivity and the financial rewards that come with it, try treating your workers as your most important asset.

---

[25] The *Innovators Catalog* is published annually by The Healthcare Forum, 830 Market Street, San Francisco, Calif. 94102.

√ Look to an established business or industry and note how they've dealt with quality and productivity issues. You don't need to reinvent the wheel.

√ Share with your peers. If the market is highly competitive in your community, call someone in the next town or state.

√ Be a proactive leader and a visionary. If you're called an idealist, consider it a compliment.

√ Create incentives that encourage others to work toward organizational goals:
  • Include medical staff.
  • Tie productivity performance into annual merit reviews of managers and staff.

√ Know what being a competent manager means and work toward it. Competent management is essential.

√ Cultivate your own management skills and then teach them to the staff:
  • Open-mindedness
  • Effectiveness in achieving results through others
  • Communication
  • Risk taking
  • Creative thinking
  • Thorough knowledge of the job
  • Honesty and integrity
  • Proaction
  • Winning attitude

√ Ask yourself, every time an idea is considered, "What's in it, ultimately, for the patient?"

√ Acknowledge (always), and compliment staff on, a job well done!

√ Other ideas: _____

_____

_____

_____

_____

And . . .

Remember to

be positive, be creative, be flexible, be terrific, be inquisitive, and
be brave!

Putting Your Staff Experts to Work:
Brainstorms & Bizarre Ideas

Because the staff holds the key to many locked treasures of innovation, the task and challenge of management becomes one of (1) finding the treasure; and, then, (2) getting it out in the open, where it can be used and enjoyed, and its benefits derived.   Sometimes, staff members may not even know their potential for participating in, and generating ideas for changes, and won't, until they try brainstorming and talking over ideas with each other. Their potential is unlimited; and the manager, as their leader, is the one responsible and able to facilitate the evolution. Undoubtedly, all staff members will be surprised at what notions pop up when bizarre or serious ideas are tossed out. But also, it is amazing to look at the results that occur when there is a conducive environment and support for creative, innovative, even bizarre, thinking.

Facilitating this environment is not difficult; but, at first, it might take a bit of nerve for the manager. If the manager has already practiced participative management, getting staff members involved will be easier. For the most part, it is a matter of setting the climate. This is done through the provision of (1) time for the staff to participate in idea-generating sessions; and (2) a comfortable, convenient place to meet. In addition, it is helpful to explore different methodologies for gathering ideas so there are a variety of approaches. These may include ongoing observation, teams, brainstorming, suggestion boxes, and also input from the staff themselves. As important, the manager and the staff must allow for failures and false starts without getting discouraged and frustrated. This process should be fun and can be done with little effort. If the atmosphere is accepting and positive so that the staff is comfortable taking risks and sharing its ideas, then there's no reason why it shouldn't be fun, creative, and productive!

Section 7

Glossary of Formulas & Data Collection Forms

Throughout this workbook there have been discussions and plans for achieving both productivity and quality in the most efficient and effective manner available to the manager. Too often, quality is seen as an intangible, unmeasurable circumstance that leaves healthcare managers with only gut feelings to document budgetary needs. The budget, as the fiscal year's plan, is the most powerful tool available to managers seeking sufficient staffing and can be instrumental in securing the necessary resources (labor, supplies, equipment) to achieve quality-based productivity goals.

Statistics Can Help

Whenever possible, workload, acuity data, staff efficiency, and other key information must be quantified or recorded so that statistical[26] trends can emerge. The "numbers," though initially unattractive and meaningless to the caregiver, should not be tossed aside lightly. As long as the numbers support patient care or the delivery of a related service and help identify or document what is needed to provide a desired level of quality, then the time spent with the calculator is certainly worth it.

The intent of this chapter is to summarize a number of formulas that healthcare managers may come across or wish to use during their careers. It's an index that can be used by experienced managers, but it is also a teaching section from which the new learner can learn concepts and some of the "how-tos" by reviewing the

---

[26] In case you're feeling faint at the sight of this word...this is not like the class you had in college. These statistics provide information that documents labor requirements, patient care and related service acuities, improved efficiencies, etc. They are significant, worthwhile, and easy and should be included as part of the normal routine in every department.

formulas and the pertinent definitions. They are ordered according to the way they build on each other, as opposed to alphabetically, (1) to assist and encourage new learners to jump in and try some of them and (2) to show the relationship of each formula to other calculations. In addition this section serves the experienced manager as a review and a reference manual.

Sources of Information for Data

Monitrends
In-house management reports
Review of reports
Special studies
Hospital associations
JCAHO
Certificate-of-need (CON) reports
State and federal government
Demographic data
Professional associations

Personal observation
Regular staff meetings
Departmental statistics
Infection control reports
State and local health authorities
Health system agencies
Professional journals
Opinion surveys
Professional organizations (e.g.,
    American Cancer Association,
    American Heart Association)

General Statistics

Total Modalities Completed:

Total number of individual modalities completed during a particular period. The length of the period is usually a month, annual quarter, or fiscal year.

Total Patients:

Total number of individual patients seen during the period, including both inpatients and outpatients. In some departments, "overlap" patients, who were first seen during the previous period but are still being seen when the new period begins, are tracked. This is useful information for departments that want to know *average modalities per patient*.

Average Modalities per Patient:

	TOTAL PERIOD MODALITIES	÷	TOTAL PATIENTS		AVERAGE MODALITIES PER PATIENT
Example #1	1,000	÷	250	=	4.0
Example #2	1,000	÷	200	=	5.0

Total Patient Days (for inpatient units):

The number of room charges posted for the period, or the sum of the daily census each day of the month. A patient may accrue 3 days in June and 4 days in July during one 7-day stay. Business office count will vary from department count if (1) patients are not properly charged for each patient day or (2) patients are admitted and discharged during the period in between the standard times the charges are posted to individual patient bills.

Total Bed Days (for inpatient units):

	AVAILABLE BEDS	X	DAYS IN MONTH	=	TOTAL BED DAYS
Example #1 (May)	45	x	31	=	1,395
Example #2 (June)	45	x	30	=	1,350

Percent Occupancy (for inpatient units):

	TOTAL PATIENT DAYS	÷	TOTAL BED DAYS	=	% OCCUPANCY
Example #1 (May)	1,000	÷	1,395	=	72%
Example #2 (June)	1,000	÷	1,260	=	79%

Average Length of Stay (for inpatient units):

	TOTAL PATIENT DAYS	÷	PATIENT(S)	=	AVERAGE LENGTH OF STAY
Example #1	100,000	÷	20,000	=	5 days
Example #2	20	÷	1	=	20 days

Average Daily Census or Volume:

	TOTAL MODALITIES OR PATIENT DAYS	÷	DAYS IN MONTH	=	AVERAGE DAILY CENSUS OR VOLUME
Example #1 (May)	1,000	÷	31	=	32.3
Example #2 (June)	1,000	÷	30	=	33.3

Budget Targets

Annual Direct FTE:

The full-time equivalents (FTE) devoted to hands-on care of the patients or providing a service. Example is based on 1.0 approved hours per modality (HPM).

PROJECTED VOLUME	X	DIRECT HPM (STANDARD)	÷	2080	=	ANNUAL DIRECT FTE
11,000	x	1.0	÷	2080	=	5.3

Annual Nonproductive FTE:

The full-time equivalents required to cover the average benefit hours (hours paid but not worked) of the direct FTE. The number of hours varies per position and institution.

DIRECT FTE	X	AVERAGE BENEFIT HRS PAID/FTE	÷	2080	=	ANNUAL NONPRODUCTIVE FTE
5.3	x	232	÷	2080	=	.6

Annual Fixed FTE:

Full-time equivalents devoted to indirect patient care or related services. As a rule, they remain constant regardless of volume. Examples are: managers, clerks and clinicians. It is a total of the desired positions, not a formula.

MANAGER	+	7-3 CLERK AND RELIEF	+	3-11 CLERK	=	ANNUAL FIXED FTE
1.0	+	1.4	+	.6	=	3.0

Annual Total FTE:

The sum total of direct, nonproductive and fixed FTEs and the total positions approved or full-time people covered by budgetary funding.

DIRECT FTE	+	NONPRODUCTIVE FTE	+	FIXED FTE	=	ANNUAL TOTAL FTE
5.3	+	.6	+	3.0	=	8.9

Total Paid Hours per Modality:

TOTAL FTE	x	2080	÷	PROJECTED MODALITIES	=	TOTAL PAID HPM
8.9	x	2080	÷	11,000	=	1.7

Average Direct Care Hours per Modality:

Ideally, direct hours per modality (HPM) are time studied and valued directly. If you want to know the HPM currently budgeted for in your department, use this formula:

DIRECT FTE	x	2080	÷	PROJECTED MODALITIES	=	AVERAGE DIRECT CARE HPM
5.3	x	2080	÷	11,000	=	1.0

Average Total Salary Costs per Modality:[27]

TOTAL ANNUAL SALARY BUDGET	÷	PROJECTED MODALITIES	=	AVERAGE TOTAL SALARY COSTS PER MODALITY
$187,000	÷	11,000	=	$17.00

Budget Targets as Productivity Measures

Actual Total HPM (Example is a 4-week period):

TOTAL HOURS PAID	÷	ACTUAL MODALITIES	=	ACTUAL TOTAL HPM
1640	÷	2,000	=	.8

TARGET HOURS	−	ACTUAL HOURS	÷	TARGET HOURS	=	% OVER (UNDER) BUDGET TARGET
1.0	−	.8	÷	1.0	=	(20%)

Actual Direct HPM (Example is a 4-week period):

TOTAL HOURS PAID	−	NONPROD. HRS PAID	−	FIXED HOURS PAID	=	ACTUAL DIRECT HOURS PAID
1640	−	160	−	480 (3 FIXED x 160)	=	1000

DIRECT HOURS PAID	÷	ACTUAL MODALITIES	=	ACTUAL DIRECT HPM
1000	÷	2,000	=	.5

TARGET HPM	−	ACTUAL DIRECT HPM	÷	TARGET HPM	=	% OVER (UNDER) BUDGET TARGET
1.0	−	.5	÷	1.0	=	(50%)

[27] Any dollars or hours can be calculated on a **per modality** basis by dividing the dollars (shown above) or hours in a given period by the modalities that accrue during the period. The same is true for FTEs. If the annual salary budget for 8.9 FTEs is $187,000, then the **salary cost per FTE $21,011.**

Actual Total Salary Costs per Modality (Example is a 4-week period):

TOTAL ACTUAL SALARY COSTS	÷	ACTUAL PERIOD MODALITIES	=	ACTUAL TOTAL SALARY COSTS PER MODALITY
$20,000	÷	960	=	$20.83

TARGET COSTS	−	ACTUAL COSTS	÷	TARGET COSTS	=	% OVER (UNDER) BUDGET TARGET
$21.50	−	$20.83	÷	$21.50	=	(3%)

Percentage Rate of Absenteeism (Example is a 4-week period):

$$\frac{\text{TOTAL ABSENCES IN PERIOD}}{(\text{TOTAL ANNUAL FTE X WORKDAYS IN PERIOD})} \quad X \quad 100 \quad = \quad \% \text{ ABSENTEEISM}$$

$$\frac{15 \text{ ABSENCES IN 4 WEEKS}}{(26.7^* \text{ x } 20 \text{ [4 WEEKS x 5 DAYS]}) = 534} \quad X \quad 100 \quad = \quad 2.8\%$$

* Given information

FTE per Occupied Bed:

TOTAL HOSPITAL FTE	÷	AVERAGE DAILY CENSUS (ACTUAL)	=	FTE PER OCCUPIED BED
550.0	÷	160	=	3.4

Ratio of Hours Worked to Hours Paid (Example is a 4-week period):

TOTAL HOURS WORKED	÷	TOTAL HOURS PAID*	=	HOURS WORKED TO PAID RATIO
3,872*	÷	4,207	=	92% OF WORKED HOURS ARE PRODUCTIVE

* Data available from payroll system or department.

Percentage of Filled Positions:

NUMBER OF FTE HIRED	+	TOTAL AUTHORIZED POSITIONS	=	% FILLED POSITIONS
24.3	+	26.7	=	91%

Overtime Rate:

OVERTIME HOURS PAID	+	TOTAL HOURS PAID	=	OVERTIME RATE
125	+	4640	=	2.7%

Forecasting

Forecasting Workload:

MODALITIES FOR LAST 12 MONTHS	X	% ANTICIPATED INCREASE/DECREASE	=	PROJECTED MODALITIES
10,000	X	1.10 (10% INCREASE)	=	11,000

Forecasting the Staffing Budget:

See annual direct FTEs, annual nonproductive FTEs, annual fixed FTEs, and annual total FTEs under the "Budget Targets" section.

Forecasting the Revenue Budget:

TOTAL REVENUE*	+	TOTAL MODALITIES	=	REVENUE PER MODALITY
$2,200,000	+	11,000	=	$200

* This is usually given information from the business office.

Forecasting the Direct Expense Budget:

TOTAL SALARY EXPENSES	$187,000.00
SUPPLIES:	
MED/SURG (LFY* = $12,000 ÷ 10,000 MODALITIES) + 7% INFLATION	14,124.00
OFFICE (LFY = $4,500 FOR 10,000 MODALITIES) + 12% INFLATION	5,544.00
MISCELLANEOUS (NO FORMULA, ATTACH JUSTIFICATION OF ALL COSTS)	2,500.00
DUES AND SUBSCRIPTIONS (NO FORMULA, TOTAL COSTS)	150.00
TRAVEL AND EDUCATION (NO FORMULA, AS REQUESTED AND APPROVED)	1,400.00
EQUIPMENT RENTAL (MONTHLY FEE x 12 MONTHS)	1,200.00
REPAIR AND MAINTENCE (ASK MAINTENANCE TO PROVIDE AN ESTIMATE)	1,300.00
TOTAL EXPENSES	**$213,218.00**
PROJECTED EXPENSE PER MODALITY ($213,218 ÷ 11,000 MODALITIES)	**$19.38**

* LFY is the abbreviation for *last fiscal year*. During that year, $1.20 was spent per modality ($12,000 ÷ 10,000). Assuming during the upcoming year the same will be spent per modality plus inflation, then: (11,000 modalities x $1.20 x 1.07 = $14,124).

Accuracy in Forecasting
(Examples are for one fiscal year.)

Workload Accuracy:

(ACTUAL - FORECASTED WORKLOAD)	÷	FORECASTED WORKLOAD	=	% OVER (UNDER) TARGET
(12,000 - 11,000 = 1,000)	÷	11,000	=	9% OVER BUDGET TARGET

Staffing Accuracy:

(ACTUAL - BUDGETED STAFFING)	÷	BUDGETED STAFFING	=	% OVER (UNDER) TARGET
(28.3 FTE - 26.7 FTE = 1.6 FTE)	÷	26.7 FTE	=	6% OVER BUDGET TARGET

Expense Accuracy: ───────────────────────────────

(ACTUAL - FORECASTED EXPENSES) ÷ FORECASTED EXPENSES = **%** OVER (UNDER) TARGET

($623,588 - $581,578 = $42,010) ÷ $581,578 = **7.2%** OVER BUDGET TARGET

Revenue Accuracy: ──────────────────────────────

(ACTUAL - FORECASTED EXPENSES) ÷ FORECASTED EXPENSES = **%** OVER (UNDER) TARGET

($2.4M - $2.2M = $200,000) ÷ $2,200,000 = **9%** OVER BUDGET TARGET

Productivity Formula

Optimal Productivity: ──────────────────────────

(QUANTITY + QUALITY) ÷ (LABOR + MATERIALS + EQUIPMENT) = **OPTIMAL**
(OUTPUTS)   (INPUTS)   **PRODUCTIVITY**

Forms Appendix

Although the glossary of formulas hopefully will prove to be useful as a resource tool for healthcare managers, it's too cumbersome to use for routine data collection. Key information has been put into a more workable format, as shown in the data collection forms on the following pages. Each form is first shown with a filled-in example and then as a blank format for copying and use.

However, keep in mind that one person's vital piece of information may be meaningless to another; so, after you have taken the data collection forms out, consider tailoring them to suit your specific needs. Otherwise they may become too long, or worse, be looked on as irrelevant, potentially diluting the very point you want to make. All of the forms are intended to be self-explanatory tools, but a brief introduction for each follows.

Form 7.1 - Data Collection Record: Patient Days

This is a general, all-purpose format for collecting data that are relevant to an inpatient unit. Although the book has focused on outpatient, service, and modality-based departments, inpatient departments, obviously, play a key role and generate statistics that are valuable to all other departments in the organization. The reader can work back through **Patient Day Log,** shown above the example of the form, to practice some of the formulas that are written on the form and see where some of the information can be found. This is a two-part process: (1) Setting up and recording in the log book and (2) gathering and analyzing the data. Patient days can be counted manually on the log sheet; but it's much easier just to call business office personnel. Also by doing so you can double-check your count. Whenever possible, write the formulas on the form. That way completion of the form can be delegated to a clerical person.

Form 7.2 - Data Collection Record: Modalities

This is a general, all-purpose format for collecting data that are relevant to all other departments that provide patient care or related services. The reader can work back through **Modality Log,** shown above the example of the form, to practice some of the formulas that are written on the form and see how the data are tracked and where they can be found. Again, this is a two-part process: (1) Setting up and recording in the log book and (2) gathering and analyzing the data. Modalities can be counted manually on the log sheet; or, if a computer system is in place, you might be able to make arrangements with the business office to receive computer printouts. By doing so you can double-check your count. Whenever possible, write the formulas on the form. That way completion of the form can be delegated to a clerical person.

Form 7.3 - Absence &Activity Report

Absenteeism is one of the largest contributors to low productivity. No matter how wonderful particular employees may be, when they are absent their productivity is zero.[28] One of the more productive things managers can do is let their staff know how they feel about the abuse of sick time: (1) It is being inconsiderate of

---

[28] An enlightening idea from Frank Stump, Director of Personnel Services, Baptist Hospital of Miami, Miami, Florida.

peers; (2) It is expensive to the organization and to the employee as it affects both the individual's merit increase and financial survival should a serious illness be encountered in the future; and (3) It, and absence abuse in general, is being watched carefully for patterns and misuse.

The **Absence & Activity Report** provides an open, nonaccusatory look at the patterns of absence in a department. The patterns for a department can be compared from period to period, or patterns for one department can be compared to those of other departments, if that is significant. If the organization has a computerized payroll system, or even if it has a system that collects payroll data manually for each employee by name, the comparison will take only a short time to compile if done at the end of the period. Because it documents data, it forces the manager to be objective[29] and can also be used as an informational message to the staff. It is interesting that the staff usually gets away with saying things to the cunning abuser that the manager could never say. Because they are the ones who have to train a float or work short in the abuser's absence, they may feel it becomes their prerogative.

Form 7.4 - Budget Expense Justification

In the formula section, under the formula for Forecasting the Direct Expense Budget, the miscellaneous category had a note regarding an attachment justifying all costs in that category (refer to page 105). This is one format that can be used. The idea is simple. At budget decision time, top management has many decisions to make. Sometimes, to save time or to be fair, a senior manager might make an across-the-board budget cut of 10%. In one department it might not be difficult to cut 10% off their budget;[30] in another,there might be a significant impact on quality as a result of budget-cutting measures.

Ideally, one of these forms should be completed for each of the expense categories, and reviewed and approved (with initials), or denied, before the budget calculation cycle. Even if you don't turn them in, it helps you plan what it will cost to achieve your department objectives for the next fiscal year. The focus is to

---

[29] Sometimes it seems like an employee is absent a lot, when they are not and vice versa; but the numbers bring us back to reality. Circumstances surrounding the absence, such as spending 8 hours trying to cover it, tend to play tricks on our objectivity. It always pays to see the facts first, before taking action.

[30] A fellow manager I once worked with bragged how he always asked for twice as many budget dollars as he really needed. And in response, the budget committee always automatically cut his budgets 50%. There is no substitute for managers having a reputation of credibility. It's worth its weight in budget dollars.

keep it simple and short, giving yourself only one sentence to convince your boss that you must attend the seminar in Hawaii next January. Writing four pages of rhetoric won't help; it will just keep your boss from reading any further to your other budgetary requests. So make it easy for your supervisor and also for yourself. After the fiscal year begins it makes a terrific log for keeping track of expenditures and making sure business office personnel are charging expenses to the correct accounts.

Form 7.5 - Budget Analysis Worksheet

After budgets are approved and the new fiscal year gets under way, some managers find themselves with a rather large pile of papers containing important pieces of budget information scattered throughout. It's always good management to collect those items of information, whether they are the same as the ones on this form or different, and put them together into one piece of paper. (You might want to make several copies and put them in different project folders, so they are at hand when needed.) It also serves as an opportunity for the manager to look over the planning that has been accomplished for the upcoming year, and evaluate it in light of what occurred this year and in light of the objectives for the upcoming fiscal year. Finally, through a few simple mathematical calculations, several key quality and productivity indicators emerge to be used as a point of comparison throughout the upcoming fiscal year.

Patient Day Log

Admission Date	Time	Room	Name	Acct. #	Principal Diagnosis	Origin	DRG Code	Disc. Date	Patient Days
5/27	9:00	4A	1	54120	HEAD INJURY	Floor	4	5/28	1
5/29	16:00	7C	2	65484	CAD	OR	17	6/2	2 + 2
5/31	13:45	8D	3	64839	MI - CAD	OR	etc.	6/3	0 + 3
5/31	03:00	9B	4	48583	FRACTURE - LEFT HIP	ED		6/21	0 + 21
6/2	09:30	5C	5	etc.	PULMONARY EDEMA	Direct		6/20	18
6/2	07:00	4A	6		MI	Floor		6/7	5
6/3	10:00	7B	7		GUNSHOT WOUND - HEAD	ED		6/9	6
6/4	17:45	2A	8		GI BLEEDER	ED		6/17	13
6/8	12:30	7D	9		CHOLECYSTECTOMY	OR		6/9	1
6/9	14:00	1B	10		CAD	CCU		6/11	2
6/10	08:00	3B	11		PULMONARY EDEMA	ED		6/21	11
6/10	04:30	3C	12		DRUG OVERDOSE	Direct		6/12	2
6/11	14:50	3A	13		CAD	OR		6/15	4
6/12	10:30	4D	14		GI BLEEDER	Direct		6/18	6
6/19	18:00	5C	15		CAD	OR		6/23	4
6/20	11:30	5A	16		MI *(Overflow from CCU)*	CCU		6/22	2
6/23	17:30	8B	17		CAD	OR			7 +
6/23	11:45	4B	18		OVERDOSE	ED		6/25	2
6/25	22:30	5B	19		MULTIPLE INJURIES	ED		6/26	1
6/25	12:30	7A	20		MULTIPLE INJURIES	ED			5 +
6/26	18:30	5D	21		GI BLEEDER	Direct		6/30	4
6/27	11:45	8A	22		RESPIRATORY DISTRESS	Floor		6/30	3
6/28	23:30	9C	23		PULMONARY EDEMA	Floor			2 +
6/29	11:45	4A	24		FRACTURE - RIGHT HIP	CCU		7/1	1 + 1
6/30	23:45	5A	25		GI BLEEDER	Floor			0 +

Data Collection Record

═ Patient Days: ═

1. Total Patients: _____ *(Include overlap patients remaining from previous month)*

2. Origin:

    ICU _____   ED _____   DIRECT _____

    CCU _____   OR _____   OTHER _____

3. Total Patient Days: _____ *(For overlap patients, include only days in this month)*

4. Total Bed Days: _____ *(Formula: Days in month x Number of Beds on Unit Total)*

5. Occupancy: _____ % *(Total Patient Days + Total Bed Days in Month)*

6. Length of Stay (Average): _____ **days** *(Total Patient Days + Total Patients)*

7. Length of Stay (Total): *(For overlap patients, in this section, use entire length of stay)*
    1-3 days _____   **4-9 days** _____   **10 days and over** _____

8. Average Daily Census: _____ *(Total Patient Days + Total Days in the Month)*

9. Direct Cost per Patient Day: $_____ *(Total Direct Expense for the Month + Total Patient Days) Total Direct Expense = $ 25,000*

Form 7.1-Example

Data Collection Record

UNIT: _____   MONTH/YEAR: _____   AVAILABLE BEDS: _____

═ Patient Days: ═══════════════════════════

1. Total Patients: _____ *(Include overlap patients remaining from previous month)*

2. Origin: ICU _____   ED _____   DIRECT _____
　　　　　　　CCU _____   OR _____   OTHER _____

3. Total Patient Days: _____ *(For overlap patients, include only days in this month)*

4. Total Bed Days: _____ *(Formula: Days in Month x Number of Beds on Unit Total)*

5. Occupancy: _____% *(Total Patient Days ÷ Total Bed Days in Month)*

6. Length of Stay (Average): _____ **days** *(Total Patient Days ÷ Total Patients)*

7. Length of Stay (Total): *(For overlap patients, in this section, use entire length of stay)*

　　　　1-3 days _____   **4-9 days** _____   **10 days and over** _____

8. Average Daily Census: _____ *(Total Patient Days ÷ Total Days in the Month)*

9. Direct Cost per Patient Day: $ _____ *(Month's Total Direct Expense ÷ Total Patient Days) Total Direct Expense = $ 25,000*

Form 7.1

Modality Log

DATE	IN PT.	OUT PT.	STAFF	ROOM NO.	PT. NAME	A	B	C	D	E	F	G	AA	BB	CC	DD
						(X 4 HOURS)							(X 5 HOURS)			
6/1	X		JOHN	201	1	X	X	-	-	X	-	-	-	-	X	-
6/1	X		JOHN	206	2	-	-	X	-	-	X	X	-	-	X	X
6/2	X		SCOTT	435	3	X	-	-	-	-	-	-	-	-	-	-
6/4		X	JANE		4	-	-	-	X	X	X	-	-	X	-	-
6/9		X	JANE		5	-	X	X	-	-	-	-	-	X	X	-
6/10		X	MARY		6	X	-	-	-	-	-	-	X	-	-	-
6/10		X	MARY		7	-	-	-	-	-	X	X	-	-	-	X
6/10		X	MARY		8	X	X	-	X	X	-	-	-	-	-	-
6/12		X	SCOTT		9	-	X	X	-	-	X	-	-	-	-	-
6/13		X	JOHN		10	X	X	-	-	-	-	-	-	-	-	X
6/14		X	JOHN		11	-	-	-	X	-	-	-	-	-	-	-
6/15		X	MARY		12	-	-	-	-	-	X	-	X	-	-	-
6/16		X	MARY		13	-	-	-	-	-	-	-	-	X	-	-
6/18	X		SCOTT	223	14	-	-	-	-	-	-	-	-	-	x	X
6/23	X		JOHN	407	15	X	X	-	-	X	-	-	-	-	-	-
6/23		X	JOHN		16	-	-	X	-	-	X	-	X	-	-	-
6/23		X	JOHN		17	x	-	-	-	-	-	X	X	-	-	-
6/24	X		SCOTT	423	18	-	-	-	-	X	-	-	-	-	X	-
6/24	X		SCOTT	210	19	-	-	X	X	-	-	-	-	-	-	-
6/25	X		MARY	214	20	X	X	-	-	-	-	-	-	-	-	-
6/26	X		JANE	219	21	X	-	-	-	-	-	-	-	-	-	-
6/26	X		JANE	416	22	X	-	-	-	-	-	-	-	-	-	-
6/26		X	JANE		23	-	-	-	-	-	-	-	X	-	X	X
6/27		X	MARY		24	-	-	-	X	-	-	-	X	-	-	-
6/28	X		SCOTT	420	25	-	-	-	-	X	-	-	-	-	-	-
6/28	X		SCOTT	425	26	X	X	X	-	-	-	-	-	-	-	-
6/29		X	JOHN		27	-	-	X	-	-	-	-	X	X	-	-
6/29	X		JOHN	215	28	-	-	-	x	X	-	-	-	-	-	X
6/30	X		MARY	419	29	-	-	-	-	-	X	-	-	-	X	X
6/30	X		MARY	407	30	-	X	X	-	-	-	-	-	X	-	-

Data Collection Record

═ Modalities: ═

1. Total Patients: _____   **Inpatients:** _____   **Outpatients:** _____

2. Total Procedures:

    A___ B___ C___ D___ E___ F___ G___ AA___ BB___ CC___ DD___

3. Hours Worked: 4-hr procedures ____ 5-hr procedures ____ Total ____

4. Average Hours Worked per FTE: _____ *(All staff work full time)*

5. Total Direct Expense: $_____ *(Staff are the only expense at $6.00 per hour)*

6. Direct Expense per Procedure: 4-hour $_____   5-hour $_____

7. Average Direct Cost per Patient: $_____

Data Collection Record

UNIT: _____   MONTH/YEAR: _____

Modalities:

1. **Total Patients:** _____   **Inpatients:** _____   **Outpatients:** _____

2. **Total Procedures:**

     A ___   B ___   C ___   D ___   E ___   F ___   G̲

     AA ___   BB ___   CC ___   DD ___

3. **Hours Worked: 4-hr procedures** ____ **5-hr procedures** ____ **Total** ____

4. **Average Hours Worked per FTE:** _____ *(All staff work full time)*

5. **Total Direct Expense:** $_____ *(Staff are the only expense at $6.00 per hour)*

6. **Direct Expense per Procedure: 4-hour** $_____   **5-hour** $_____

7. **Average Direct Cost per Patient:** $_____

8. **Hours per Modality:**

     Budgeted _____   **Classified/Required** _____   **Actual** _____

Form 7.2

Absence & Activity Report

Dates of Study _____

Unit/Department _____

Name	Full-time or days worked per week	Paid Sick or Absent Days	Unpaid Sick or Absent Days	Total	On Week-end	With Week-end Day Off	Days Off Worked	Over-time Hours Paid	Odd or On-call Shifts
7-3									
J. Greenfield	FT	0	0	0	0	0	0	0	0
E. McClure	FT	4	0	4	3	1	9	72	3
C. Todaro	3	0	0	0	0	0	7	0	0
D. Blair	4	1	0	1	0	1	2	0	0
R. Meghan	per diem	0	2	2	2	0	8	0	8
N. Bond	FT	0	0	0	0	0	0	0	0
Y. Kieval	FT	8	0	8	0	8	0	0	4
3-11									
J. Jones	FT	2	1	3	0	0	3	24	3
S. Tumarkin	FT	0	0	0	0	0	0	0	0
D. Russell	FT	1	0	1	0	0	1	8	1
J. Karaboyas	per diem	0	0	0	0	0	6	0	7
A. Lawrence	3	0	0	0	0	0	4	0	3
2 Shift Total		16	3	19	5	10	40	104	29

Form 7.3-Example

Absence & Activity Report

Dates of Study _____
Unit/Department _____

Name	Full-time or days worked per week	Paid Sick or Absent Days	Unpaid Sick or Absent Days	Total	On Week-end	With Week-end Day Off	Days Off Worked	Over-time Hours Paid	Odd or On-call Shifts

Form 7.3

Budget Expense Justification

Department ___*Surgery*___   Cost Code ___*672*___   Prepared by ___*J. V. Jones*___

Expense Category	Item	Cost	Justification and Use	Approval
4	*General Office*	*$9,000*	*$1.00 per modality*	
4	*Calculator (1)*	*$70*	*Budget calculation*	
4	*Videotapes (20)*	*$200*	*Video taping/patient charge*	

EXPENSE CODES:	1 - purchased services	4 - office supplies	7 - med-surg supplies	10 - food
	2 - other supplies	5 - miscellaneous	8 - travel/education	
	3 - equipment rental	6 - dues/subscriptions	9 - department repairs	

Form 7.4-Example

Budget Expense Justification

Department _____   Cost Code _____   Prepared by _____

Expense Category	Item	Cost	Justification and Use	Approval

EXPENSE CODES:	1 - purchased services	4 - office supplies	7 - med-surg supplies	10 - food
	2 - other supplies	5 - miscellaneous	8 - travel/education	
	3 - equipment rental	6 - dues/subscriptions	9 - department repairs	

Form 7.4

Budget Analysis Worksheet

Department __*Emergency*__ FY __*88*__ HPM __*1.5*__ Prepared by __*D. Kranz*__

Staffing Pattern

		Current FY	Upcoming FY
Total	RNs	10.0	12.0
Total	EMTs	3.0	4.0
Total	LPNs	1.4	2.0
Total All Staff		14.4	18.0
Total Fixed		3.0	3.0
Total Nonproductive		1.6	2.0
Total Department FTE		19.0	23.0

Direct Expenses

	Current FY	Upcoming FY
Total Salaries	$ 395,200	$ 502,320
Total Office Supply	$ 5,000	$ 5,500
Total Med-Surg Supply	$ 10,000	$ 11,000
Total Repair/Maint.	$ 6,000	$ 6,000
Total Misc./Ed./Other	$ 2,000	$ 2,500
Total Direct Expense	$ 418,200	$ 527,320

Unit of Service

	Current FY	Upcoming FY
Projected Modalities	20,000	25,000
Flexible (Direct) Hours per Modality	1.5	1.5
Weighted (Total) Hours per Modality	3.0	3.0

Monitoring Information*

	Current FY	Upcoming FY
Supply Expense (cost) per Modality	$ .75	$ .66
Salary Expense (cost) per Modality	$ 19.76	$ 20.09
Other Expense (cost) per Modality	$ .40	$ .34
Total Expense (cost) per Modality	$ 20.91	$ 21.09

* For "per unit" costs, total the expenses in a category and divide by the annual modalities.

Form 7.5-Example

Budget Analysis Worksheet

Department _____ FY ____ HPM ____ Prepared by _____

Staffing Pattern	Current FY	Upcoming FY
Total _____	_____	_____
Total _____	_____	_____
Total _____	_____	_____
Total All Staff	_____	_____
Total Fixed	_____	_____
Total Nonproductive	_____	_____
Total Department FTE	_____	_____

Direct Expenses

	Current FY	Upcoming FY
Total Salaries	$_____	$_____
Total Office Supply	$_____	$_____
Total Med-Surg Supply	$_____	$_____
Total Repair/Maint.	$_____	$_____
Total Misc./Ed./Other	$_____	$_____
Total Direct Expense	$_____	$_____

Unit of Service

Projected Modalities	_____	_____
Flexible (Direct) Hours per Modality	_____	_____
Weighted (Total) Hours per Modality	_____	_____

Monitoring Information*

Supply Expense (cost) per Modality	$_____	$_____
Salary Expense (cost) per Modality	$_____	$_____
Other Expense (cost) per Modality	$_____	$_____
Total Expense (cost) per Modality	$_____	$_____

* For "per unit" costs, total the expenses in a category and divide by the annual modalities.

Form 7.5

Roey Kirk is a noted expert in healthcare management. Using her own experiences from 11 years in both managerial and administrative positions in a 513-bed, community hospital and 5 years as a management consultant, she has developed systems that organize and simplify nursing, clinical, ancillary, and support management functions.

As a consultant, adjunct university instructor of applied management, and seminar leader, Roey Kirk has helped many individuals and organizations make the most of their healthcare management staff. She believes that quality and productivity can exist side by side, and that individual departments can make a positive impact on a hospital's profitability. Using time-tested teaching and training methods, candor, and understanding she shows readers, students, and workshop participants that proactive management skills are not a gift that some are born with, but a set of techniques that can be easily learned, adapted, and used.

Roey Kirk has a bachelor's degree in sociology, a master's degree in management, and is a member of the American College of Healthcare Executives. She has written many articles for healthcare management journals and lectured at many programs nationwide for healthcare managers, administrators, and executives. She has published several books on healthcare management including:

- *Nursing Quality & Productivity: Practical Management Tools (1986)*
- *Nurse Staffing & Budgeting: Practical Management Tools (1986)*
- *Identifying Costs & Pricing Nursing Services: Practical Management Tools (1987)*
- *Healthcare Quality & Productivity: Practical Management Tools (1988)*
- *Healthcare Staffing & Budgeting: Practical Management Tools (1988)*
- *Quality-Based Costing, Pricing & Productivity Management for Home Care Organizations (1988)*

She is president and owner of Roey Kirk Associates, management consultants, in Miami, Florida.